LYRICAL IOWA

2019

The Seventy-fourth Annual Anthology
of

THE IOWA POETRY ASSOCIATION

www.iowapoetry.com

Affiliate Society
of
The Academy of American Poets
and
The National Federation of
State Poetry Societies, Inc.

Marilyn J. Baszczynski, Editor

Copyright by
The Iowa Poetry Association
2019

Fusebox One Printing
Grimes, IA 50111

ISSN-0076-1699

This edition of *Lyrical Iowa* is dedicated
to all who write, read and enjoy poetry,
but especially to the memory of the following
Iowa Poetry Association members whose death
we have learned of since publication
of the 2018 book.

Gretchen Fosket
November 1, 2018

Howard P. Johnson
December 9, 2018

Larry Lenfred Link
December 31, 2018

In addition to its many large and thriving cities, Iowa's countryside is dotted with over nine hundred smaller communities that many residents as well as businesses choose to call home. Whether the community grew around businesses establishing a presence in a new area, or whether new business opportunities arose as a result of the skills and needs within an existing community, the prevalence of this duality is clearly visible in many of our rural towns, like the one pictured on the cover. Each has its own story and, depending on your information source or vantage point, there may be more than one side to the story they have to tell.

Photographed in Redfield, Dallas County.

Photo taken by Chris L. Baszczynski

TABLE OF CONTENTS

Dedication 2

Iowa Poetry Association Past Presidents 4

From the Editor 5

President's Message 6

Contest Judges 7

Acknowledgements 7

Iowa Poetry Association Officers 8

Area Representatives 8

Members of IPA 9

Contest Rules 11

Adult General Poems 13

    First Time Entrant 18

Humorous Verse 116

Sonnets 120

Haiku 127

National/World Events 134

Poems FOR Children 138

    Gretchen Fosket Memorial Award 138

College 148

High School 152

Upper Grades (5-8) 162

Lower Grades (K-4) 169

Index 175

IOWA POETRY ASSOCIATION
PAST PRESIDENTS

1945 -	AGNES FLANNERY, Des Moines
1949 -	RAYMOND KRESENSKY, Algona
1950-1953	GRACE HUNTER, Grinnell
1954 -	MAUDE T. WALROD, Des Moines
1957 - 1959	THOMAS F. DUNN, Des Moines
1959 - 1961	MARY ALICE HART, Creston
1961 - 1964	LOUIS A. HASELMAYER, Mt. Pleasant
1965 - 1967	PEARL J. MINOR, Mason City
1967 - 1969	FRANKLIN GROOMES, Menlo
1969 - 1971	CAROLYN JORDAN, Des Moines
1971 - 1973	ALETHA HUMPHREYS, Toleda
1973 - 1975	ELEANORA MILLER, Leon
1975 - 1977	MAX BARKER, Marshalltown
1977 - 1979	LUCILLE E. MORGAN, Des Moines
1979 - 1981	WILL C. JUMPER, Ames
1981 - 1982	LOREN C. GRUBER, Indianola
1982 - 1985	PAT KING, Albia
1985 - 1988	RALPH SPEER, Des Moines
1988 - 1992	LOREN C. GRUBER, Clarinda
1992 - 1996	PAT KING, Albia
1996 - 2000	DAVID STOKESBARY, Gowrie
2000 - 2004	BILL RUDOLPH, Grinnell
2004 - 2008	RONALD H. KAHL, Burlington
2008 - 2011	JERRY L. FERRELL, Des Moines
2011 - 2014	DENNIS D. MAULSBY, Ames
2014 - 2016	MARILYN J. BASZCZYNSKI, Earlham
2016 -	JERROLD NARLAND, Winterset

FROM THE EDITOR

These past months, I have enjoyed traveling through the lyrical stories of hundreds of Iowa poets, each wanting to share a small part of their universe. Within these pages, readers can explore a five-year-old's dreams of riding a rocket to the sky, or a 95-year-old's assurance of love's triumph over time. Other poems call on readers to writhe with animals through paintings, or maybe race with them across Iowa landscapes; there are poems that lament loss, replenish hope, give voice to what is not easily shared. In considering the many experiences and beliefs that lead poets to write, US Poet Laureate Joy Harjo's statement comes to mind, that "poetry is the voice of what can't be spoken, the mode of truth-telling when meaning needs to rise above [...] everyday language." It is my privilege to share these voices here.

A quick look at the numbers—the 2019 Lyrical Iowa Competition brought in 865 eligible entries in Adult General, 38 in Humorous Verse, 45 in Sonnets, 35 in National/World Events, 137 Haiku and 60 Poems for Children for a total of 1,180 poems. In the Student Division, eligible submissions included 50 College, 251 High School, 257 Upper Grade (5-8) School and 97 Lower Grade (K-4) for a total of 655 poems. The present volume includes 381 poems, chosen from these 1,835 entries, with contributions coming from well over one hundred cities and towns across 77 of Iowa's 99 counties, and with authors of all ages and from all walks of life.

I'd like to welcome our first-time entrants and those who have signed up to become IPA members! My suggestions to all poets, from novice to experienced: attend a workshop (info at www.iowapoetry.com), join a poetry group, check out NFSPS contests, attend and participate at readings. Keep writing…I and many others will be reading…

Thank you to our Associate Editors for their many hours of careful reading, sorting and selecting. A special thank you to Lucille Morgan Wilson for her constant encouragement and always welcome advice.

Marilyn Baszczynski, Editor-in-Chief

SPECIAL NOTE: You may notice that there are two poems included for Robert Wambold of Council Bluffs. This is due to my oversight in last year's anthology; his poem was mistakenly omitted from the 2018 edition, so I have included it here along with his selected poem for 2019. My apologies to Robert.

PRESIDENT'S MESSAGE

It is with much pleasure that I am able present to you the seventy-fourth edition of *Lyrical Iowa*. Within its covers, you will find some of the finest poetry our state has to offer. The styles, subjects, and voices offer such amazingly broad ranges that it is hard to imagine any reader being unable to find a poem that strikes a special chord within them.

The poems presented in this volume have been selected by the judges from a much larger field of entries and, in their opinions, comprise the cream of the crop. I have found it difficult to open to any random page and not find at least one poem to my liking. I hope you will find it the same.

Jerry Narland
(IPA President 2016 -)

Visit the **Iowa Poetry Association** website at

www.iowapoetry.com
for information on:

Membership
Current Contest Winners
Semi-annual Workshops
Past Editions of *Lyrical Iowa*

2019 CONTEST JUDGES

Adult
    General — William D. Reyer, Tiffin, OH
    Humorous Verse — Ann Gasser, West Reading, PA
    Sonnets — Ralph Speer, Colbert, WA
    Haiku — Stan Malless, Murphy, NC
    National/World Events — Ann Gasser, West Reading, PA
    Poems FOR Children — Lisa Toth Salinas, Spring, TX
College — S Stephanie, Rollinsford, NH
High School — Nynke Passi, Fairfield, IA
Grade School — Budd Powell Mahan, Dallas, TX

ACKNOWLEDGEMENTS

The Iowa Poetry Association gratefully acknowledges the following special gifts and thanks those whose generosity helps to support our contests:

- <u>Adult General</u> category prizes co-sponsored by the family of **Edna Bacon Morrison**, Associate Editor of *Lyrical Iowa* from 1965-1971 and a long-time active member of IPA. Also co-sponsored by **Jerrold Narland**, sitting IPA President.

- <u>National/World Events</u> prizes given in his memory by the family of **Carl Stiefel.**

- <u>Poems FOR Children</u> , an investment gift of **William Godfrey.**

- <u>Humorous Verse</u> prizes provided by **Maxine Carlson** in memory of **Margaret Siskow**.

- <u>Sonnet</u> category prizes, a bequest from the estate of **Vivian Buchan.**

- <u>Haiku</u> underwritten by **Margaret Westvold**, in memory of a dear friend and poet, **Dorothy Fyfe**.

- <u>Special Award for a First Time (adult) Entrant</u> provided by **Shelly Reed Thieman**, in honor of all the poets gone before us, and in celebration of those with whom we still work..

- <u>Gretchen Fosket Memorial Award,</u> in grateful recognition of Gretchen's many years of dedicated service to IPA, provided by **Alpha Poetry Group,** of which Gretchen was also a member.

- <u>Student prizes</u> are funded from the **Albert Lyell & Jauvanta M. Walker** Endowment Fund, by memorial gifts from family and friends of **Virginia Blanck Moore** and by a bequest of **Marie Jacobsen**.

OFFICERS & EDITORIAL STAFF

Jerrold Narland, 122 S. 7th Avenue, Winterset 50273 ....President
Max Molleston, 2271 E. Grantview Dr, Coralville 52241......................First Vice President
Maxine Carlson, P.O. Box 2360, Iowa City 52244..........................Second Vice President
Margaret Westvold, 1318 Duff Ave., Ames, IA 50010..Secretary
Linda S Harris, 711 Sixth Street SE, Altoona 50009 ....Treasurer
Shelly R Thieman, 1120 24th St, West Des Moines 50266 ....Communications
Marilyn J Baszczynski, 16096 320th Way, Earlham 50072 ....Editor-in-Chief
Heather Derr Smith, 2709 Walnut St, West Des Moines 50265 ....Associate Editor
Steven WE Rose, 306 W 1st Ave, Indianola 50125................................Associate Editor
Rustin Larson, 105 North D, Fairfield 52556..College Editor
Joy Lyle, 17844 330th St, Keota 52248 ....High School Editor
Della Weems, 32944 K Ave, Adel 50003..Grade School Editor

AREA REPRESENTATIVES

Adair - Margery Watts
Adams - Sharon Becker
Audubon - Lori Shannon
Black Hawk - Lori Culbertson Harris
Boone - Margot Conard*
Bremer - Dennis Sanborn
Buchanan - Michael Andorf
Carroll - Lori Shannon
Cedar - Michael Andorf
Clarke - Sharon Becker
Dallas - Margery Watts
Des Moines - Rodney Reeves
Fayette - Dennis Sanborn
Franklin - Margaret Flint Suter
Greene - Margery Watts
Grundy - Jean M Evans*
Guthrie - Margot Conard*
Hamilton - Margot Conard*
Hardin- Kay Jons Roelfsema

Howard - Marjorie Dohlman
Jefferson - Barbara Bloom
Johnson - Max Molleston
Lucas - Sharon Becker
Mahaska - Pamela Blomgren
Marion - Jay Immel
Mills - Jane Chamberlain Oksasky
Mitchell- Ramona Morse
Muscatine - Duffy De France
Page - Jane Chamberlain Olsasky
Scott- Mike Bayles
Shelby - Jane Chamberlain Olsasky
Story - Dennis Maulsby
Van Buren - Dale Nethertoni
Woodbury - Jayne Vondrak
Worth - Marjorie Dohlman

* stepping down in 2019. We thank them for many years of service in promoting our efforts at IPA.

2018-2019 PATRONS

Elizabeth Janvier Abramowitz
Joyce Allen
Janine Ambrose
michael h andorf
Ethel Barker
Marilyn Baszczynski
Patricia K. Bieber
Judith Bienfang
Sarah Ruen Blanchard
Pamela J. Blomgren
Norbe Birosel Boettcher
Lloyd E. Brockmeyer
J. Kay Brown
Patricia H. (Pasha) Buck
Dan Campion
Maxine Carlson
Lynn Cavanagh
Joseph W. Chambers
Kathleen Christy
Shelley Jones Clark
Jean C. Conover
Janice C Down
Debra S. Downey
Shea Doyle
Susan R. Drake
Tracy Edens
Lee Sterling Enslow
Jean M. Evans
Gretchen Fosket"
Thomas Georgou
Peggy A. Golden
Lee L. Gordon
Kathleen M. (Kass) Harper
Linda S. Harris
Phyllis I.T. Harris
Randy Hengst
Kay L. Herring
Robert M. Hinnen
Lorene Hoover
Mark Huddleston
Mary Jedlicka Humston
Linda S Jacobs
Deborah Johnson
Howard P. Johnson*
Ronald H. Kahl
Barbara J. Kalm
Terry D. King

Karen Kladivo
Frank J. Kutchen
Cheryl K. Larsen
Rustin Larson
John K. Lerdal
Deborah A. Lewis
Phyllis North Lewis
Joy Lyle
Gerald W. (Jed) Magee
John McBride
Charles W. McKenny
Mary E. McManus
Belinda H Merritt
Jeffrey Scott Meyer
Kathleen M. Meyer
Joe Millard
Douglas L. Miller
Liz Lynn Miller
Pauline Miller
John Mitchell
Rebecca L. Moad
Wally Moll
Max Molleston
Marjorie W. Moore
Lisa Morlock
Ramona Morse
Virginia R Mortenson
Jonathan JT Moss
Jerrold J. Narland
Gene L. Needles
Dale Netherton
Patricia E. Noeth
Mary D. Noffke
Nancy Obermueller
Ginnie Padden
Jim Quinn
Delia Ralston
Rita F. Reed
Warren Robert Reinecke
Janet McMillan Rives
Margot Rupp
Rosemary Sackett
Dennis Sanborn
Larry H. Schroeder
Norma T. Schroeder
Martha J. Schut
Mary Shaw
Linda L. Shivvers
Mark Stellinga

Fred Stiefel
Carroll Stokesbary
David Stokesbary
Janis K. Stone
Betty Taylor
Shelly Reed Thieman
Denise Tiffany
Misty Urban
Pamela J. Vincent
Jayne Vondrak
Richard K. Wallarab
Margery L. Watts
Ina Waugh
Bradley Weidenaar
Margaret Westvold
Rebecca Whitmore
Lynn Wielenga
Lucille Morgan Wilson
Mike Wilson
Carol H. Winter
Norman G Wolfe
William Woodhouse
Steven C. Woolery

* Deceased

2018-2019 MEMBERS

Patricia Albin
Mark Armstrong
Ali Arsanjani
Lila L Andersen
Margot Bannister
Oma Bauge
Mike Bayles
Sharon R. Becker
Jo Ann Benda
Diana Benzing
Judith Bienfang
Michelle R. Black
Janice L. Blankenburg
Barbara Bloom
Pauline Borton
Joyce A. Branson
Betsy Brant
Jody Bresch
Christine Brink
Roger Brockshus
Phoebe Bubendorfer
Barbara B. Cardamon
Linda Marie P. Carlson
Heather Ann Clark
M. Wayne Clark
Alanna R. Clutter
Margot H. Conard
* Lorene M. Conner
Kathryn Corones
John H. Crabb
Margaret Crawford
Beverly Crouter
Joneva Currans
Maryam Daftari
Doris Daggett
William J. Dall
Duffy DeFrance
Irvin Deichman
Sandy Deyoe
Marjorie K. Dohlman
Linda Dolphin
Vicky L. Dovenspike
Jean Hagert Dow
Theresa Durkin (Hogan)
Adriene (AJae) Egger
Kay R. Eginton
Rose Elsbecker
Julie S. Emmons
J. Michael Entz
Elaine M. Erickson
Angela A. Evans
Janelle R. Finke
Deborah M. Finney

Mike Fladlien
Elaine Tweedy Foley
Bonnie L. Forey
Deb Fowler
Shirley Franklin
Phyllis L. Frazier
Edy Fudge
Leslie Ann Gentry
Milli Gilbaugh
Janet Gilchrist
Mary Kay Gleisner
Emma Lee Godfrey
Bill Graeser
Beverly Mattix Green
Karl R. Green
Phyllis L. Green
Sandra L. Green
Jeffrey Grimes
Nancy Grudens-Schuck
Marcia Haakenson
Grant Halsne
Nancy J. Hanaman
Bonnie B Hanlin
Richard L. Hanson
Lori Culbertson Harris
Kathleen G. Hart
Brian Haymond
Viola Hill
LeAnn Hoeg
Dolores Horton
Ann Hudilainen
William E. Hudson
Michelle Hunt
Jay Immel
Pam Jarvis
Elizabeth Johnson
Julie Allyn Johnson
Richard L. Johnson
Carole A. Johnston
Sandy Keller
Susan Klein
Heather Knowles
Sandra Conner Ladegaard
Mary Jane Lamphier
Mary Martin Lane
Teresa Lawler
Elizabeth A. Leick
Phyllis North Lewis
Nancy Samcoe Link
Larry Lenfred Link*
Kelcy Lofgren
Mark S Lucas
Helen E. Lyness

Phyllis A Lyte
Dorothy Mathis
Mary Ann Mathis
Elaine Mattingly
Dennis D. Maulsby
Les McCargar
David L. McCoid
Carol McMullen
Maxine McNeil
Betty C. Medema
Gloria R. Milbrath
Sandy L. Moore
Barbara Morrison
Melba Muhlenbruch
Linda Muller
Rosella Myles
Merle E. Newman
Anna M. Nicholas
Judy D. Nolan
Stephanie Novotny
Jane Chamberlain Olsasky
Louise Opheim
Catherine W. Opper
Kate Ortiz
Robin Ostedgaard
Frann Ostroff
Dawna Page
Carole Pannhoff
Linda Paul
Nancy J. Peters
James M Proudfoot
Joan Rammelsberg
Richard Ramsey
Rodney G. Reeves
Lauren Rice
William Riddle
Nancy Riggan
Lucy Ringold
Lynn Rae Robbins
Hollie Roberts
Kathryn Jons Roelfsema
Gene M. Rohr
Donna Rupp
Kathleen Russell
Paul C. Sabelka
Theresa Sager
James K Sandin
Myrna J. Sandvik
Joanne Dyhrkoop Schar
Karen Schmitt
Chris Schultz
Richard Sears
Lori Shannon

Mary Arlene Shaver	Janet Thomas	Janet Wiener
Robert Shaw	Barbara Thompson	Steven & Mary Wikert
Jacqueline Signori	Steven T Thompson	Sharon Witty
Carol Sisterman	Jean B. Thomson	Linda Wolfe
Janet F Skiff	Jodie Toohey	Shirley Wyrick
Phyllis L. Skinner	Adele K. Turner	Martha Yoak
Dawn Sly-Terpstra	Pat Underwood	Sally Young
Andrew J Smith	Marvin D. Vallier	Mary L. Zachmeyer
Lindsey Smith	Donna J Wallace	Danielle Zimmerman
Margaret Smolik	Michael D. Walsh	Lynne D. Zotalis
Robin Sprafka	Joan Jessen Waske	John P. Zuckerman
Audrey Stromberg	John L. Weaver	
Marie E. Sullivan	Val Weaver	* Deceased
Margaret Flint Suter	Lois E Wessels	
Susan Swift	Virginia Westbrook	
Bryan Tabbert	Barbara Wheeler	

Lyrical Iowa 2020 Competition
General Rules for All Divisions

Contests are open to all persons with Iowa residence (See College exception). No entry fee. No membership or book purchase required. Poems must be original and unpublished, including on-line and self publication. Poems must be submitted by their author, except for student poems, which may be submitted by student, teacher or parent. Vulgarity or pornography is NOT accepted. Up to 5 poems may be submitted by one author. All poems except haiku must have titles. 20-line limit unless otherwise specified. Line limits do not count title nor spaces between stanzas. Lines should not exceed 60 characters or editor may make arbitrary line breaks and count them as separate lines. Send poems after January 1, 2020 to editor for your division. **Deadline: February 28, 2020.** Winners and others to be published in Lyrical Iowa 2019 will be notified as soon as all judging and poem selections are completed (mid-summer). No one will receive more than one award. No more than one poem will be printed per author. IPA has first publication rights; all other rights automatically revert to each author AFTER our publication in late fall. No simultaneous submissions. Poems may not be withdrawn after submission.

Note new 75th Anniversary Adult Category for 2020.

ADULT - Email all poems together in one email copied into the body of the email. NO ATTACHMENTS. Include name, address, phone #, county and indicate if first-time entrant. Indicate category at top of each poem. Send to **contest@iowapoetry.com**.

If you DO NOT HAVE EMAIL, each poem must be on separate 8 1/2 x 11 sheet of paper. In upper right corner include name, address, phone #, county, poem category and if first-time entrant. Mail together in #10 envelope . Include SASE for contest results. No registered mail. Send to Marilyn Baszczynski, Editor, 16096 320th Way, Earlham IA 50072

Prizes: Decision of judges is final. Prizes will be withheld in cases of plagiarism and in any category where inadequate entries are received. Cash prizes offered are as follows:

- General category: (any subject, any form, 20-line limit) $100, $60, $40
- Haiku: (traditional English 5-7-5 nature, includes time/season implication):
- $40, $25, $15
- Sonnet: (any recognized sonnet form, 14 lines): $40, $25, $15
- National/world Events: (any form, 20-line limit) $25, $15, $10
- Poems FOR Children: (written by adults, suitable for reading to or by children. any form, 20-line limit): $25, $15, $10
- Humorous Verse: (8 lines or less, must be rhymed & metered): $25, $15, $10
- **Special 75th Anniversary:** (anniversary subject, any form, 20-line limit):$75

   Honorable mentions are awarded in each category. Prizes may be increased by board action and additional memorial awards may be made.

COLLEGE - Email all poems together in one email copied into the body of email. NO ATTACHMENTS. Include name and location of your school, your name, home address and email. Send to **rlarson@mum.edu**, with IPA COLLEGE POETRY CONTEST as subject line. If you do not have email, mail paper entries (see ADULT instructions) to Rustin Larson, PO Box 1721, Fairfield, IA 52556. Graduate students should enter the Adult Division. Prizes: $25, $15, $10.

SCHOOL CONTESTS - Must include 1) author's name, 2) home address, 3) grade in school, 4) teacher's name, 5) name and mailing address of school, 6) teacher or parent email address in upper right corner. One poem per sheet. Some school poems will be selected to go on to next year's national competition. (**No email submissions**.)

   HIGH SCHOOL (grades 9-12):
   Send entries to Joy Lyle, 17844 330th St., Keota, IA 52248.
   Prizes: $20, $12, $8.

   GRADE SCHOOL (grades K-4 and 5-8 are judged separately):
   Send entries to Della Weems, 32944 K Avenue, Adel, IA 50003.
   Prizes: $15, $8, $5 in each section.

FIRST PLACE, ADULT GENERAL:

POLLOCK'S MURAL

Crow black and teal twists,
slither in vertical
lines that dominate the medium.

Brindled blood red and rouge,
waterfalls of sulfur dioxide yellow
and ivory semaphores foreshadow death.

A decaying dolphin agonizes for air.
A horse's head mocks from Andalusian depths.
A brother's skull floats in an aureole of Aegean blue.

Energetic and rhythmic,
anguished and elated,
vibrant and quiescent.

Enormous and magnificent
as the Claíomh Solais sword.
Rare as snow drifts on the Sahara.

Delia Ralston
Waterloo

DEATH OF A CLOWN

He was a jug-eared fool, a clown of old school,
    The court jester and village friend.
With paint on his face and collar-ruffle lace,
    He had at last come to joke's end.

Of him that remains were his dusty cremains
    And two of his comic duck calls.
His total life-earn rested in a big urn,
    Along side his juggling balls.

It was he who chose to wear a rubber nose.
    He was a comic – not a clown.
But folks hearing his name, recalled his great fame,
    A recollect of his renown.

Dan Moore
Davenport

SECOND PLACE, ADULT GENERAL:

SHIFT: PLUNGE
after Psalm 42

Deep calls to deep at the roar of your waterfalls;
All your breakers and your ways have gone over me.
"Deep calls to deep" supersedes suicidal ideation.
Deep calls to deep, and deep answers: roar,
tumult, baptismal purge – dumb urge toward suffocation
dies; living submission arises as breath. No longer gunshot
but ocean's roll and roar, no longer freefall but rip current
into mightiest love, no longer rip but pierce and stitch;
self-impalement hesitates; pointed patient search
ensues; no longer drowning, but – no longer mere
drowning! Deep calls to deep, and foam and force
of torrent, joyful, severe, soda, steel wool,
rush alive to scour the base and inside of the skull,
unravel heart tissue, untangle veins, arrange anew and raw,
revive. It's a descent into death, all right – twisted wish
overpowered, drowned, scoured, rerouted, risen, rinsed.

Allison Boyd Justus
Ames

ALONE

I am sailing with my father. We share an easy silence.
A gentle breeze brushes my skin and water slaps the boat.
He steers the boat through the water then asks me to take the tiller and I sail.
Wisps of fog blow across the bow then thicken.
Do you want to take over I ask,
You're all right he answers and I sail on.
The boat slips silently through the dark water,
and I turn to him but he is gone......
I grip the tiller and slack off the main sheet.
My chest tightens, my breathing ragged.
The fog thins, the sails flap.
I swallow hard and sail.

Susan Klein
Waterloo

THIRD PLACE, ADULT GENERAL:

RACING

Teeth chew copper-laced steel	Walk
Power floods two travel as one	Trot
Muscles flow under fiery coat	Canter
Strong slender fingers curl in wind-snarled mane	Gallop
Hooves dig deep in moist black earth	Gallop
Damp leather aroma mingles with green alfalfa buds	Canter
Callused hands caress sweat-flecked neck	Trot
Warm breath murmurs my best boy	Walk

Robin Sprafka
Winterset

WHITE BOARD: TIMELINE

A wood slab dressed in peeling white paint
  patches gaping hole of her treehouse.
White surfboard under arm, adventure rapid in veins,
  she runs through the sand an eye on ocean surf.
Arms interlaced, they traipse the white hanging bridge
  to the lighthouse: their first night together.
She returns for 25th school year to remodeled art room--
  a whiteboard means no chalk dust at day's end.
A congregation sings Amazing Grace and shares memories
  in a country church, a white clapboard structure.
She paints the sky blue on a white timeline.

Kathleen Stauffer
Osage

FIRST HONORABLE MENTION, ADULT GENERAL:

ICE FEVER

Whenever my brains boil over the brim
of my ten-gallon hat and my mouth singes
dad's badge-shiny face, he points me
to straddle his fresh cake
of ice tethered inside the walk-in cooler.

"Riding this three-hundred-pound white stallion
sweetens any sour tongue," my sheriff orders.

My wet chaps on the western trail soon wrinkle
as I fidget and squirm, slouch
and slither on my swale saddle,
nearly toppling

into a low-riding parked dolly of stacked metal cases
filled with half pints of fresh whole milk.

My sass quickly cools
when dad enters with his holstered ice pick
and honed-sharp tongs to free

blocks of ice for the morning's hot route,
while I ride, waiting for dry pants
like any spanked wrangler

ready for a hot lunch in the bunkhouse.

Dick Stahl
Davenport

FRUIT OF MY LIFE

You're the apple of my eye.
And the peaches in my pie.
You're the bananas in my bread.
And the berries in my spread.
You're the cherry on my sundae.
And the watermelon on a hot day.
You're the oranges in my juice in the morning when I awake.
And the strawberries in my shortcake.
You're the honey from the bees.
And the mango in my smoothies.
A love so sweet shall never die.
You'll always be the apple of my eye.

Tami Anderson
Cedar Rapids

SECOND HONORABLE MENTION, ADULT GENERAL:

THESE HANDS

These hands do the work of a miller
These hands do the work of a slave
These hands do the work of a carpenter
These hands do everything but dig my grave

These hands have been raised in anger
These hands have been offered in love
These hands many times have seen danger
These hands have asked for strength from above

These hands are stiff in the morning
These hands sometimes ache at night
These hands will never complain
These hands turn the darkness to light

These hands, they are not pretty
These hands are lined with age
These hands, they ask for nothing
These hands can still turn the page

These hands, these hands, these hands

Kelly Clute
Center Point

THIRD HONORABLE MENTION, ADULT GENERAL:

THE TASTE OF LOSS

I tasted your ashes.
I had licked the flavor of you from my fingers
So many times before.
The grit of you,
The soft sandy dust of you
As you lifted into the wind.
As ever, you lingered on my touch.
Bringing you to my mouth was as natural as breathing.
Our good-bye kiss gray with memory.
Smoky granules of your bones passed between my fingers,
Lingered on the web of my thumb and forefinger
As I pointed you toward eternity,
Upended the urn,
To tap out the last, powdery thought of you.

Margaret Flint Suter
Hampton

SPECIAL AWARD, FIRST-TIME ENTRANT:

SUNRISE PANTOUM WITH A SHRINKING SISTER

Everything looks bigger in the winter:
the bus more full with the inflated body
of coats, hats that grow heads taller than hair.
Beautiful stacks of snow pushed aside liberates

the bus more full with the inflated body
I still carry. Even the smoke looks
beautiful. Like stacks of snow pushed aside. Liberate
the memory of hills she and I sledded together

that I still carry. Even the smoke looks
ordinary in the camera's lens. I try to capture
the memory of hills we sledded together,
even the pink streaking strands of clouds

ordinary in the camera's lens. I try to capture,
but everything is always yellowed here—
even the pink streaking strands of clouds.
Sometimes people tell me I look lighter now,

but everything is always yellowed here—
on coats, hats that grow heads taller than hair.
Sometimes people tell me I look lighter now,
but everything looks bigger in the winter.

Crystal Stone
Ames

THE MAN WHO LOVED THE NURSING HOME

he exists, it's not a dream
in large gray sweats, matching top and bottom
a long beard and a story
happy for a home
and helping hand, if you can't be home
this is not a bad place, he said
you search his eyes for a lie
no one could possibly ever believe that
one side is useless, he says, and demonstrates
in case you lacked faith in his conviction
but it's not for you to decide
you are a guest in his house

Shea Doyle
De Witt

INTERESTED

I am interested in being interested.

I wonder about the word 'wonder'.
Ex. You are a wonder
Because of your magnanimity, your sweetness.

I wonder about the infinite possibilities between
The numbers 100 and 200,
Or 10 and 20,
Or 1 and 2—
[There is space between and space between the space between…]

Wondering is accessed only by a mind as interested in
Wondering as it is wondering about being interested.

I am interested in lenses.
The lens through which I view the sidewalk or
My mother/A flower/A war memorial,
Anything and all things.
Are these lens photographing and storing,
Are they preserving and memorizing,
Is there any difference between a conscientious view and an idle view?
I am interested in being conscientious
Not always but most of the time.

Matilda SC Mackey
Iowa City

TRIBUTE: FOR MARY OLIVER

Under winter walnut, I gather nuts,
figments and fragments, to squirrel away
for summer day when hummingbird
cha-chas over pink lantana.

Maybe on that faraway afternoon,
I will crack the tough shell
and dig out meat to feed my spirit.
Maybe on that distant day,
I will turn to the blank page
and welcome shadowy ghosts
lingering outside my door, begging
entrance into diaphanous light.

Perhaps today, as birch logs
crackle and crumble, I will clutch
your poetry to my heart and let
wild, precious lines waken my muse..

Jayne Vondrak
Kingsley

ONEIDA STREET

I was seven years old the first time I heard a gunshot.

I'd waited for my parents to turn off their bedroom light
before quietly stacking my dolls under my arms to continue
my play by the glow of the streetlamp in the living room.

Three shots were fired.
Rubber screamed against cement.
Three beats of silence and then sirens.

I don't remember the sound of glass shattering,
but the bay window from the house catty-corner from
my own was scattered across the lawn.

My father ran into the room and I waited for
the furrowed brow and demand of an explanation.
His anger never came.

The doorbell rang and my mother jumped.
A tired policeman sat in our living room,
one restless foot crushed the arm of my doll.

My mother brought him coffee
and he asked questions
I didn't know how to answer.

Lauren Petri
Cedar Falls

MOUSE

The mouse knows
from the get go
he's small.

That there's many
a mouth bigger
than he,

which can swallow him
in a snap—with or
without his tail.

So he runs
wherever he goes,
never lays in the sun
or lingers by the cheese.

Yet, no less than the cat
or the fox, the mouse
fills his belly
and sleeps.

Bill Graeser
Fairfield

LOT'S WIFE

Wouldn't you look back?
Wouldn't you want a memory?

Maybe she yearned for the places
where she bore her children, the
little stream where she joined
her sisters to gossip, to bathe
in cool water, nurse her babies,
gather herbs for cooking.

Maybe she tired of her husband's
zealotry, his stubborn faith in an
unseen god. Maybe the angels
irked her, their dire warnings, their
commands to flee, to forsake friends,
family, all she had ever known.

I'll never get to heaven. I'll never
hear how her story ends. But if you
get there, will you look her up? Will
you kiss her salty hand and bless her?

Will you give her my regards?

Jean C Conover
Mapleton

AND SO SHE DID

She bemused me when our eyes passed
Amused me with her deep grin
Confused me as I
Wondered that

Such a bold young woman

Could
With little effort
Permeate my heart,
Saturate my being,
Inundate my whole life
In a second

That became a lifetime

And so she did.

Robert Shaw
Dubuque

ALL ON A SUMMER'S DAY

Bright blue sky, sun's up early
Barefoot dance in dewdrops pearly
Blackbird feasts in mulberry tree
Red, red robin sings merrily

Halter tops, hula hoops
Soda shops, ice cream scoops
Front porch swing, lemonade
Ginger cookies mama made

Cotton candy, county fair
Concert band plays in the square
Night crawlers, cane poles
Tire swings, swimming holes

Youngster captures firefly
Pyrotechnics in the sky
Moonlight, starlight
Who's afraid of the ghost tonight?

Disc jockey, street dance
Beckon summer romance
Embrace these moments as you may
Money can't buy—a summer's day.

Audrey Stromberg
Ames

BUSY NIGHT

A dock laden with children barking at the bats
Backs flat as slats dig but who can move
There is a whirl in the swoosh overhead

Stars chasing the wisps over waves
Pink orange yellow fades with dark fingers chasing
Bluish is captured by the tip toe of black

Slapping waves fade into flicks
The night breeze whispers and fish frantically flop
Bats become specks as tree tops entice

Ground flickers flirt with aerial fireflies
The call of their wild slingshots children to shore
Frantic swoops of flurry to capture light

Karen Kladivo
Mount Vernon

VIOLET

I'm always one to take an idea
and run with it
so that's what I did
after Leonard drank the last of my jar money
for the millionth time
one final gasp of Coors and cigarettes

got one of those tracksuits
lavender shiny stuff shifting
as I walker down the block
had Trudy at the shop do my hair the same
Egyptian queens for my ears
wedding ring in the jar

decades of hiding my coins
trips to Topeka extra pocket pinned inside my skirt
now tube socks hide my stash
and marigolds keep me company

Sister says I am a woman
who knew how to widow long before I'd need to
I say I am a woman
who knows how to eat a butterscotch and enjoy it

Sandy Deyoe
Des Moines

GHAZAL

Will someone please buy my rainbow?
No. It's impossible to sell a rainbow.

My brother does push-ups on stage.
Above him is a paper rainbow.

He is in The Pirates of Penzance.
Who are the cops? Where are their rainbows?

How could the daughters all be the same age,
Dancing, leaping under their rainbow?

In a car outside, the devil sings on the radio:
Every cop is a criminal, dire rainbows.

Venus floats directly in the west.
It is much too late now for rainbows.

The play is over. Let old Rustin tell you this much:
Cherish this endless family of strangers, this rainbow.

Rustin Larson
Fairfield

IN THIS ETHIOPIAN RESTAURANT

we're a mosaic,
the batik on the wall
where all colors drape as one.

We tear soft African bread,
gather chicken, cabbage,
green beans, mushrooms
with our fingers.

It's been fifty years since
King's death. *I have a dream!*
Glory! Glory!
   Praise the Lord!

We sip our tea,
the fragrance from the platter
succulent. Our stomachs
fill and families line up
to take our seats.

Here, there's enough equality
to sustain a future, enough
pots in the kitchen
steaming to overcome.

Pat Underwood
Colfax

DRINKING TEA IN SAN FRANCISCO

I dream of a Japanese tea garden
where I search for my father's WW2 soldier-ghost
among Shinto spirits and Zen gardens raked like ocean waves.

On pebbled paths the *kami* laugh at their tricks.
Screaming middle-schoolers on a scavenger hunt,
busloads of slow-footed senior citizens block the way.

A monument stands to master-gardener Hagiwara,
a bronze-rusted lantern given by children to mark
a message of peace to pacify wartime internment.

I drink *genmaicha* tea in bamboo shade,
brown rice bobs at the bottom.
You will meet someone important, curls atop crumbs.

I find my father's soldier-ghost in the eyes of the wrinkle-faced
woman, pouring tea, serving *arare*, grandfather Hagiwara's
hand on her heart, gentle now.

My father, also gentle, his hand deep in the sand burying
Pacific nightmares in a tin box lined with medals.

Dawn Sly-Terpstra
Lynnville

THEME PARKS

The X liked to take our brood to any Pablum place
requiring sun screen and an overnight drive or more
out of Nebraska. Disney on both coasts,
Anaheim back when the middle child still needed
my shoulders, next Orlando—then three months later
her suitcases were gone, once all our kids
were old enough for school.

Before then, Oceans of Fun the summer Bill Clinton ran
and she was pregnant with Sam. The water slides were drugs
to her. Over and over and over again, on her back,
her belly bloated like a beach ball, she'd funnel
down into my worried arms or those of any
passing stranger who, splashing by, was alarmed
about this fetus precarious as family luggage
tied by bale cord and towels to a dust bowl Ford sedan.

We'd brake her spray-legged slide and laugh with her
as one does with prophets or the soon to be departed.

Little did I know.

Steve Rose
Indianola

BOREALIS

There are eight bones in your wrist. Northern Crown
in the night sky above the birches. Yours are scattered

in the dirt. Coronation of some man's headship over you.

I'll keep these little joints from your hand I'll keep them
in my purse, in my pocketbook with this pistol, engraved

with all your names. It was all worth it. Even your blood
spilled from the gash under your rib, you would still say

It was all worth it. We will pour and pour, like fear
from Adam's mouth. I'm a partizan now and I hunt

with you in the thickets and through the crosshairs, turning
from slogans to murder and I have no regrets. What they say

about revenge is all wrong. We know this. The women who killed
went on to live a good long life, drinking brandy in the village,

the chickens running around her heart-shaped feet
                    under the shade of the apple trees.

Heather Derr-Smith
West Des Moines

WINTER SOLSTICE ENCROACHES

the aging goat feels it too
this shortening of days
omen of an end
before shifting to light

he stays indoors
nibbles bits of apple
not tempted by sweet
feed or mash

today he crunches
my peppermint candy
tomorrow I'll try applesauce
to mix with his grain

he only needs to make it
through the turn
until the days lengthen
with unquenchable appetite

Marilyn Baszczynski
Earlham

CALLED BACK
For Emily Dickinson

In the midst of things
I think of you
eating a green apple,
tying your shoelace,
drying your toes.

Your passion needed four days of silence,
a cup of tea,
a poem.

I think of you in the midst of things,
and, when my pain is more like beauty,
I know something of what it is to fall,
and be called back to sing.

John William Collinson
Fairfield

WHEN I START PAYING ATTENTION

I saw the crows first, silhouettes
against a sooty snow bank while
walking to the bus stop. Three
of them dipping their heads.

The rabbit was too intact to be roadkill.
Body unmarked, belly full, lying on its side.
Legs bent as if running. Did it freeze?
Was the cold enough for it to sleep?

Maybe the crows caught it
as it leapt into the open. Or snatched it
from its respite. The body happened
to fall where I would pass it.

But to witness crows feasting. To observe
the red divots of their beaks in the flesh.
Tufts of ashen fur scattered on the ice.
They flew as I approached.

They were there again the next day,
body and crows. If I were a different kind
of person, I might have snapped
a photo.

Caroliena Cabada
Ames

ELEGY ON A DEAD RACCOON

The body lies beside the road
A furred lump, hit by a passing car
Left like refuse, unremarked
While we in the cocoon of our car
Pass by without a second glance.
We think we are different and special
But our mammal bodies are the same:
A baby raccoon was born, suckled,
Stretched its paws, struggled to walk,
Learned to eat, to drink, to clean himself,
Wrestled with his brothers
Explored the same world we live in
With the same five senses.
But when he died
In a sudden, tragic accident
His body was left beside the road,
A furred lump.
There were no remarks at a solemn funeral
And no elegy
Except for this one.

Marty Miller
Donnellson

DESK WITH A VIEW

I just want a little desk pushed
right up next to a picture
window with a view--

of sunlight filtering through trees, specks of blue
sky like bleached sapphires, shimmering;

of an old rainbow-striped hammock, like
Joseph's coat of colors, twisted and hanging from
low branches of an apple tree;

of golden leaves scattered like lost coins, glittering
the sparsely-grassed dirt tree-skirt;

of a barn-red house with ferns and hostas and
greens of all sorts sprouting from its base,
the intersection of domesticity and wildness;

of its matching barn-red shed with cream
clapboard shutters, containing years of secrets
I'd like to know.

Rachel Kramer Hibma
Sioux Center

MOVING DAY

She knew the chill of other moves
that first day of March
when she walked the muddy lane
helping him load the truck.

Leaving behind land
leased year to year,
they crossed miles to plant seeds
in another man's field.

She held teacups wrapped in her mother's quilt
and dared to hope for wide, clean rooms,
gardens tilled in green rows
and apple-scented orchards.

On the next hill, a house shone white.
Their lane led to a porch weak
with toothpick posts, a door with torn screen
that would bite into her hand.

Other Marches, other moves
and always the white house on the hill
until, at age 92,
March first came again.

Lorene Hoover
Ames

KERNELS OF GLASS

1.
Kernels of corn fell to the earth
scattered like broken glass
fitting, nodded the farmer, just like the price of a bushel

2.
A farmer lives like a seer
looking into the future from
more than one angle

eye to eye with a rainstorm
that washes away seed
fists to fist with weeks of no rain
that grows dust at his feet.

3.
"This is my life."
He says as he pulls his boots off on the porch.
"A life of hell."

4.
Now tariffs have brought more worry
to lives steeped in anxiety.
The farmer sees all that can go wrong

and the tariffs
are another monster under his bed.

Robert Steinbach
Ankeny

MY SISTER-IN-LAW'S LIFE

Her husband died
She cried
Their young daughter and son survived

A new husband arrived
She cried
Her daughter and son revived

Her husband thrived
Melissa cried

Three new children arrived

Donnella Moss
Adel

OIL SPILL

A red-throated loon
tangled in seaweed
floats on a slick of oil
rainbows in her feathers.

Phoebe Bubendorfer
Des Moines

PERISH THE THOUGHT

skeletal arms, wind shuddered limbs stretch
from rolling hills
atop white mantle, cornfield's languid sleep
the repose of energy spent producing bounteous yield
our Mother's labor seemingly effortless, taken for granted
as seasons evolve

driftless Mississippi River bluffs birth new life in eagle's eyrie
where milkweed fairies flit
free to propagate nourishing
millions of monarchs fueling
their 3,000 mile migration from
high mountain Michoacán forests   mee' cho ah cahn
to Canada in a miraculous passage
accomplished by four generations
in mere months

some say our planet's survival is dependent upon theirs
our existence its extension
as much as air   water   earth
enough to sustain life until
it's not

Lynne Zotalis
Decorah

SEED DISTRIBUTORS (BY VOLUME)

1. wind
2. water
3. bird, a dove or maybe a lark
4. mammal
5. Dow Chemical DuPont
6. BASF "We create chemistry."
7. Syngenta-ChemChina

Levi Lyle
Keota

THE MUSIC

I sit cross-legged on thick grass carpet
Of open meadow,
My face to sun and sky.
Music is the wind
That tumbles down the mountain,
Sad-voiced violins weeping honeyed air,
Fleeing toward the soul of who
I really am.
A boiling orchestra of spirit
Gives itself to the core of who I
Wish to be
And who I may yet become.
I am old
My time is short.
But still I am.
There is yet music.
There is.

Tom Gingerich
Kalona

MELODIES

Black piano notes floated in the window
from two houses down the street

July had been in that house
The yellow one with the grand piano

Dan played
Dan, the neighborhood handyman

July wondered what would happen
to Dan and his piano if he were hurt
cleaning gutters, washing windows,
fell off his rickety red ladder

July's birthday parties would be
too quiet, in July
The piano and Dan would sit, forlorn,
broken

Life would be sucked from South Green St.

Barbara Bloom
Fairfield

SANDBAG

Water laps up to
the top of the levee. The river
front is now just the river. Citizens
line up single file, ankle deep, shoveling
sand. Building a wall against the rising water,
sand pouring from shovel to sack, an hourglass.

North the levee broke, Gulfport's gone,
a collection of bars and strip clubs washed away.
Kegs and bottles, like bath toys, float by downstream.
Defenders atop sandcastle battlements joke
It needed a good cleaning. Gallows humor
at the sight of alligator rooftops
with their dormer window
eyeballs poking out

above the current. We will be
the antediluvians, sandbagging
to keep our heads above water, staying out,
drinking late, pairing off two by two.
Waiting for the dove to return,
and the river to fall.

Justin Curran
Burlington

STORMY PARTNERS

She stands in love while
He falls in and out, over and over

His chaos is wild lightning
Her negativity thunderous darkness

He wilts standing outside her -
Solitude
Languid

His complaints are blizzards whiting out -
Appreciation
Contribution

Tornado arguments carried off her
Affection
Playfulness

After the storm,
Calm
Peacefulness

The sun will shine again
 Are they committed —
Or resigned?

Dorothy Mathis
Ankeny

BETRAYAL

You said, "Friends build bridges,
fences are deadly sin..."
So, I scared myself, dared
myself and let you in.

No secret was too sacred
for your beckoning ear;
no pain was too painful
for a new friend to share.

I shared, I bared myself;
I unlocked the fence gate...
Your friendship a façade—
I discovered too late.

No secret proved too sacred
for you to retain;
no pain proved too private
for you to contain.

You said, "Friends build bridges;
deadly sins are fences..."
So, I scared, bared, dared, shared myself,
betraying my better senses.

Marcia Haakenson
Lake View

BREAK UP
in loving memory of Gary

A sliver of ice
clings to the morning paper.
Old leaves lie
in mirrors of water.

I remember the hanging dice
in your '54 Ford, your fingers
caressing a guitar.

We traveled miles not on the map.
Have you found the gold streets
of heaven that you longed for?
My grief is a grave
of snow on my head.

We meet in a dream—you wearing
your red flannel shirt,
waving at the foot of the stairs.

Now I have only the mail's ads
I shuffle through,
the bran flakes on my spoon.
But a hint of sunlight
is draped over your wooden chair.

Elaine Erickson
Urbandale

UNDER THIS SEPTEMBER SKY

The river's ruffled by our wake.
White caplets form
like a quintet of porpoises
    surfacing.
Migrating pelicans
ride driftwood south,
    past
the tint of autumn
hugging the shore.
Scores of gulls
swoop and circle.

What is the September sky?
Clear and cloudless
reflecting color
back to the river
or cloudy gray
with bits of blue
revealed, like the opening
of consciousness
to the greater beyond.

Barbara Cardamon
Cedar Falls

BACKYARD HOUSE WREN

Oh, plain brown bird with your short tail held proud,
the weight of two quarters hopping about
your bubbly voice wakes wispy cirrus clouds.
Oh, plain brown bird with your short tail held proud.
Hammered-by-hand palaces dangle prim,
petite holes keep gossipy sparrows out.
Oh, plain brown bird with your short tail held proud
the weight of two quarters hopping about.

Lori Culbertson Harris
Cedar Falls

STOP AND LISTEN

Quiet noise of the ducks skimming
the creek.
A heron grunting as he passes over.
The pitter patter of leaves landing
on the water.
Small things that are reassuring
in their beauty.

Angela Evans
Johnston

I KNOW WHAT YOU'RE THINKING

Raised by the street
Absent Father
Can't Read
Interested in rap and sports
Speaker of Ebonics
Must be a criminal

Michael Fischels
Independence

TROUBLE

They locked me up, threw away the
key. How long before they set me free?
Will my baby remember me? I don't know I'll
have to see. How long before they're done
with me? I pray to God they let me be.
I want to leave this dog-and-pony show.
God help me I feel enraged, this Judge
got me caged. I hope justice comes
swift and fast. With my punishment comes
wrath. How long can my baby last?
I need to get home and make some cash.
I wonder what the Judge will cast on
me. Judge, no, I beg you, please,
have mercy on me.

Jeremiah Phillips
Davenport

GOLD

When the little town looked like harvest,
Teenagers set the prairie ablaze in lieu of hanging their math teacher.
Quietly the dried mire perished,
Halting slowly when it met the town's weary fire force.
"S'about time we built a billiard hall for 'em,"
Said No. 4 to No. 7,
his hands red from dedication.

Daniel Joyce
Fairfield

IN SICKNESS AND IN HEALTH

Standing there in your virginal satin and lace
Worrying about what sweat is doing to your
Carefully constructed curl and "do"
Did you listen to the "blah, blah blah, Love
Honor and blah, blah in Sickness and in Health, blah, blah
                  'til Death…blah, blah
You may now kiss the bride!!!?"
Did you mean it? You vowed it.
You meant it through Health – the passion, the adventure,
Laughing, Crying, Partnering, Parenting
Tough times and Triumphs
Did you reckon with the Sickness?
The sweater, buttoned crooked, decorated with remnants of lunch
The furnishings of Sickness - wheelchair and commode
Only one of you able to operate this new technology
As two made those vows, are you still bound by
What only one remembers now?
Shush, shush, shush ….Remember, you are
….Not Bound   ….But Blessed

                                                          Margot Bannister
                                                                       Ames

8 SECONDS AGO

Eight seconds ago you were born
or we just met or you were
seventy then 97 with translucent skin
and sagging laugh lines
closely guarding pale green eyes.
Eight seconds ago we stared at the camera
while sitting on musty ground near Pond's edge
as the amateur photographer
captured our souls ~
 a moment we shared,
 one we'd never share again.
Yesterday or seventy or ninety-seven
or just eight seconds ago
we search scattered brains
trying to find a tribute to ourselves,
where we were and weren't,
who we are and aren't,
and we chime together
"Remember when?"

                                                    Pamela J Blomgren
                                                              Oskaloosa

TIMELORD

After the explosion, before the dissipation.
White cools to color, black engulfs matter
Hydrogen fuses, galaxies collide
Photons flee at the limits of time.
Nothing is too small, everything is too big,
Perception is the only border, reality is uncharted.
Akin Odin on the wings of Huginn and Muninn,
Grab a handful of imagination and bravery
Ride them to the edge, or the center
Both are nothing, only the between holds the happening

All happenings happen, all happenings matter
Some where, some when, to some thing, to some being
Explore the happening as it happens,
It will not last.
There may be, is, will be, mourning.
There may be, is, will be, joy.
Go on, persist, endure, prevail.
Again and again, time after time
That is when you will have lived a life that matters.

Sheila Baker
Iowa City

LOSS

It's the second spring since you've gone.
My second chance to find happiness.
Another city, another country, another love.
None of these things have erased you from my heart.
I look for you around every corner.
I see your smile on someone else's face.
I see you walk far down the street
and I run to catch you.
I think of how you would have laughed
at this joke or enjoyed that tune.
Why must I see a second spring?

Patricia A Huxsol
Charles City

LIFE, A GIG

Up to perform
Sing the song
Play the tune
Fake the smile
Move along
Soon be gone

Jan Myers
Spencer

ONE FROM JERICHO

I am your Zacchaeus (and you not quite my Christ);
come dine with me. We shall sit beneath my sycamore and perhaps salvage
the leaves at our feet. But you will die because you are dust.

You cannot save me. You did not create heaven, or earth, or me.
I have fallen and you have died, unable (or unwilling) to protect me.
Could you protect me, were I widow or orphan?

My wet pleas curve the edge of your Bible.
Does it open without you now, to tell you of the king
who tore out his own bowels and threw himself from a cliff
while his people stood waiting to save him?

But you can't help me,
protect me, save me.
Everyone else but me.

If you don't love me, lie to me then, while your shadow passes.
Linda MJ Muller
Iowa City

TROUBLE ON MY MIND

I got troubles, troubles on my mind--
I worry, as democracy decays in this country of mine
I seen a baby at the border crying, tear gas in her eye
I seen a mother trying, trying to wipe those tears dry

I got troubles, troubles on my mind--
I worry, as I watch wicked men rule the world
I worry, greed is to whom their hearts are sold
I worry for the mother with no child to hold
Ripped from her arms when she wouldn't let go

I got troubles, troubles on my mind--
Let the children in, this be their home
Let the parents follow, leave neither alone
Nobody lay claim on land that claims liberty for all
Empires rise, they rise and they fall
Nolan D Nickerson
Cedar Falls

TOMMY'S GENERAL STORE

Long ago when I was a girl
We "traded" at Tommy's General Store.
A hand of bananas hung from the ceiling,
A touch of the tropics for our small town
Even when frost painted the front window.
Tommy's special saw cut one banana, or
A whole bunch if Mother had invited company.
Behind the counter row on row of canned goods
Stood in colorful labels, a beautiful sight.
Off to the side the vinegar barrel waited,
Its wooden spigot ready to fill jugs brought from home.
Sitting on the cracker barrel, Tommy's wife sang
"Alexander's Ragtime Band" as Tommy donned gloves
Before going to the back room to get kerosene
For a customer. Back there they candled eggs,
Good as cash for farm families trading
For sugar, tobacco, and a new pair of work socks.

Carol B McMullen
Webb

THE AFFAIR OF A LIFETIME

Above the grass-choked parking lot, your autograph fades;
Y blinks baffled, O stutters surprise, U yawns lazy.
N,K,E,R,and S stay out all night and celebrate The Final Sale.

Our fashionable affair spans ruffled petticoats
and saddle shoes, sequined gowns and sultry sandals,
and the latest in polyester pantsuits and slip-proof flats.
I've enjoyed your company from elegant structures
on Main Street to the crowded halls of anonymous malls.

Now with skewed devotion, I play your coupon games
and trade my paycheck for price-slashed goods sporting
yards of useless receipts, despite your dubious interest.

The decay of your hospitality dismays me:
buckets on the floor collect rain and my tears,
padlocked powder rooms and broken escalators spur
a brisk sprint to the hostess boasting the shortest long line.

Yes, I've always known that you will inhale
my withered wallet's last breath—and now my pockets
spill—one hundred coins spin a jig to your cash register's
lullaby. Our courtship dissolves with a toast and a vow:
I will find a new suitor.

Julie Sharp Emmons
Norwalk

THEY

We are offered advice
each and every day
from faceless and nameless strangers
known to us only as *They*.

Experts every one, who do we believe,
I am told some experts have no degree.

We are told how to talk and how to walk.
They tell us how to cook using recipes from a book.
They tell us how to clean
and tutor us from do-it-yourself magazines.

They tell us what to wear and tell us not to swear.
They tell us how to sit and that exercise keeps
our backsides fit!

With all this advice coming our way
I question and wonder,
just who in the heck are *They?*

Robert D Wambold
Council Bluffs

REFLECTIONS

We live and learn,
time marches on.
Past days are gone.

My grandchildren,
when they were young
wrote letters to me,
just for fun.

Shared books with joy,
baked cookies too.
Found tiny bugs,
that hid from view.

Sang songs at night
with my guitar.
Observed in awe,
a shooting star.

We learn to live
from days gone by.
They tell us 'why.'

Sue Drake
Grinnell

THE BOY

Brass shell in the dirt, arterial bloom on the saddle
the boy
Crack the reigns, keep your eye on the hills
that aint no boy, father said
Water the horses, rid your hands of blood
but he was
Stoke the fire, forget his eyes
he was younger than me
We'll forage golden streams in places he'll never see
it was him or you
Fortunes gleaming under drawers of water
still that dont mean
The creeks and rivulets holding our future
he had to die
run as swift as the crimson from his neck
his tomahawk fell
We carry on to better life
I drew my gun
Leaving him behind for the western sun.

Cory B Taylor
Cedar Falls

PLAYING IN THE BASEMENT

My friend loves to tell the story, spill blood in the water
and your heart comes running,
come close and hold her hand to see.
I see the flicker of concern in my son as in my mother:
What have you been believing now?
If you want the truth, find someone whose pulse isn't racing
to the scoop, spinning the tale of evil vs. us,
deepening the ruts, dragging all blame to one. The truth's
in the corner paying you no mind, busy with the housework,
will answer when probed, doesn't enjoy hearing itself talk.

When we played in the basement too long, we lost the sun.
We traded it below for make believe.
Too late we come out to the ending day.
In Greek truth means not-forgetting, not-oblivion,
but we didn't forget it, we walked in the wrong direction,
we stayed in the basement all day playing anger and pretend,
we had the charming but not the truthful friends.
The quiet truth-knowers already turn toward home,
too late I come
to the ending day.

Lisa Ross Thedens
Walker

CRYSTAL

drives a twelve-year-old Toyota,
manages a Casey's near I-80.

Her two teenage daughters
lost their dad in Iraq.

Two years later
she found Dan, a paramedic

who left her, thirty-two,
with a five year-old son.

An F-250 crossed the centerline,
hit his ambulance.

Chris drives a big rig,
England, Swift, now Werner.

He's four years younger and
not home much, but he loves her.

Has been sending checks
for five years to help out.

They Skype each evening, talk
about quitting the road, of marriage,

buying a house, being together,
as time eats away at their dreams.

Jerrold Narland
Winterset

THE BIG BANG

There was nothing
before the Big Bang.
Not a Little Bang.
Nothing.

Then,
one morning
standing in the sunlight,
there was you.

Floyd Pearce
Cumberland

THIS TRAIN

This train keeps chugging ever forward. There are many possible routes it can take on its journey, but it will only take one. Sometimes I control the switch for a coming junction, but more often it is completely out of my hands. There have been dark tunnels scattered along the way. Some quick to pass, some long and deep and cold. But even tunnels bring a promise of coming sunshine -- a return to bright meadows reaching out on every side and scattered with flowers and streams and misting waterfalls cascading down distant mountains. When the terrain turns rugged and harsh, there is beauty in its midst to be discovered. If the emergence from a tunnel comes at nighttime, the moon and stars are there to bear witness of open spaces. The lullaby of the rhythm of the tracks drones on and on, day and night, comforting, annoying, then comforting again. It's true that sometimes a storm may throw a tree across the tracks and our progress is slowed until the obstacle is dealt with, but once again the motion returns and the journey carries on. I don't know when or where this train will finally come into a station, but I am blessed to be riding this train with you.

Sarah A Butz
Fort Madison

MAPS

Unpredictable me,
traveling down endless roads that call.
Bricks and stones of weathered roads
mask my arduous journey.
Adversity compounds my confusion
as I roam along a tangled grid of roads
and unpaved trails.
Detours excite, yet confuse me,
as they extend the unreachable horizon.
Directions ignored,
enticed by the unknown,
I change directions without notice,
knowing one day,
I will abandon my freedom,
for maps.

Robert D Wambold
Council Bluffs

TOWARD THE "THIN PLACES"

The skin of visions, dreams is very thin.
Oh, to move more toward the "thin places"
Where the God beyond and the God within
most nearly merge;
Where the gulf between the sacred and the secular
is nearly erased;
Where the veil of mystery permits glimpses
of reality beyond mere knowledge;
Where common things hint at the uncommon;
Where the fog clears slightly between
the known and the unknowable.
Oh, to move toward the "thin places."

Lloyd E Brockmeyer
Cedar Rapids

THE JOURNEY IS DONE

The feet are the
soul of the shoes.
And without the
feet, the shoes are
an empty body,
vacant vessels that
sit in the corner,
quiet as a tombstone,
forgotten, and curled
at the toes, flowers and
grass smashed into
the tread.
The tan leather is
baked brown from the
sun, tired and cracked
from the long lonely
miles of wandering,
finally the journey
is done.

Thomas Case
Mount Pleasant

BEACH-HEADS

On this now placid shore
waves of time that pitch and roll over the past
conceal atrocities

Centuries dampen the screams of those who suffered in war
their bodies and blood commended to deep oceans and fading memories

We no longer hear plaintive voices crying out
from watery sepulchers

Only breakers pounding the sand one after another

Doom...
Doom...
Doom...

Janvier Abramowitz
Coralville

SNAPSHOT FROM AFGHANISTAN

Military outpost in the Korengal Valley

A soldier on the ledge

His head in his hands

He may be shot

on the next patrol

Duffy De France
Muscatine

COMING HOME

Humming dirges and
crushing pepper by the
biting twilight,
fireflies illuminating the
fields of grass and
smoke crawling through
my fingertips,
I feel the
bludgeoning of the earth,
the vibration of moving
soil, excavating my
lost homeland,
the last relics of my
fragmented past.

Ranelle Irwin
Kingsley

DUSK WALK

I step past a skull poking out from weeds,
a scavenger's nest of broken jaws and ribs,

remnants of animals picked clean through winter.
A farmer tills an adjacent field, breaking open earth

that smells like rain. Cars on the highway
whine a mile south and a jet stream forms overhead

with passing rumble. A cacophony of machinery.
I pause from walking to take a selfie with the Moon

and Jupiter perched over my shoulder. The Sun
quickly setting, chilling the spring air as bright yellows

and blues fall to muted pastels that blend
seamlessly while the dew settles down for slumber

and sticks to my shoes, slowing me down.
A few song birds finish discussing the day,

early risers who must get to bed in order to
wake me pre-dawn, chittering outside my window.

Shade turns to shadow as I shuffle back,
cold and weary, welcoming night.

Heather Ann Clark
Winterset

DOWNSTREAM ON PINE CREEK

The house stood empty for years,
shrouded in cottonwoods and volunteer willows.
"She took sick real sudden and never come back,"
they said. Windows, thick with dust,
used only for looking inside now.
A pan sits on a big woodstove,
dining table set with dinner plate and glass.
Sagging living room couch has a deep hollow
near closed book and cup on the end table.
Quilted throws are still draped over chairs,
and shelves full of cups, books,
and small jars that look to be empty.
Faded pictures of people in shades of brown
barely show against flowered wallpaper.
She never came back, never had time
to properly set her house in order,
leaving daily debris, the simple details
of living, as her final testament.

Douglas L Miller
Solon

GOODBYE

You left me too early my love...

I loved you...

More than the flowers love the early morning dew

More than the waves love reaching the distant shore

More than a million stars love the night sky

More than the east loves every sunrise

And the west every sunset

On an early November morning you were gone...

And I didn't get to say goodbye

JoAn N Stevenson
Decorah

LOVE HAS WON

and so time
as an ancient
moss-covered boulder
holds within its grasp
all the sunlight of its joy
the mist of its hope
and the shadow of its grief
    half realized in
    the dawn of each new day
    as
    silently
    the waters of life
    move mysteriously
        ever
            forward

Iola Powell Cadwallader
Oskaloosa

THE LITTLE THINGS

On nights when I feel lonely,
but lonely only for you,
I open the little ceramic box with violet flowers on it
where I keep the lock of hair you gave me.
I touch it, and study its blackness and shine.
Then I unfold the tee shirt that carries your scent
and take in a long breath.
I read each word on the scraps of paper
where you wrote notes and to do lists.
Sometimes these things make me smile,
and sometimes they make me weep.
They bring me closer to you,
while emphasizing the miles between us.
And I realize in those moments
that I don't even know how
to love someone as much as I love you.

Anna Nicholas
Cedar Falls

LOVE'S VIGIL

It's ten o'clock and there's a dog barking nearby
The skin of your arm is pressed against mine
Both of us quietly sitting close, knowing why
Words unspoken at just the right time
Never forgetting love's hopeful promise
Requires constant vigilance to survive
The warmth of your arm grows more intense
As your lips press softly against mine

It's three o'clock and the whirling of a fan serenades
A sleepless hour that passes by in record time
Recalling the day, before wakefulness fades
Moments seemingly ordinary, now sublime
As you lie next to me I cannot help but think
There i no other place I would rather be
When daylight breaks and the morning sings
Your tight embrace welcomes me

Robert M Hinnen
Dubuque

WHALE OF HEARTBREAK

I am blue on blue
ready any second to
jump the gun begin again
another false start.
So Sanpaku my pathology
sticks like glue.
I'm just too big blue
floating on a lovely atoll
blue mud puddle blue-muddled.

Martha Yoak
Iowa City

METEORS AND MORNING GLORIES

I couldn't have asked for more in a meteor.
It came in—a long slow pitch, clearing the roof
and ending in the trees.

You told me about the morning glories—
her favorite—that climbed up to
the second story window of your bedroom.

Sometimes reassurance and encouragement
come as a home-run meteor in the August sky
or a blue flower face in the morning.

Trudi Rosazza
Iowa City

rose

we sat hard
cloudy eyed
staring ahead
for clues

while kind folks
with prayers
soft landed
on fears

as last night
a stolen rose
left a garden
in tears

David Hasenmiller
De Witt

THE SCHOLAR

He stacks words like a juggler
twirling plates atop a pole:
ethos, pathos, logos, kairos.
Like taffy, he twists and tugs them into shape,
rolling them beneath his tongue—
chewing, savoring, swallowing.

In his classroom, words of civic discourse march
in silvery lines against a field of black,
fearless philosophers battling positing politicians.
"Amō, amās, amat, amāmus," chant his students,
their conjugations elbowing chaos into order
like drumbeats reverberating inside one's head.

Dictionaries edge his windows like drapes
while newspapers skirt his tables and chairs.
He prays in Latin with his village priest,
trades news in German over the bakery counter
and orders gelato in Italian at the sidewalk cafe.
Neighbors, smiling, recall his many tongues.

This man who is remembered is . . .
a man of words—and more.

Judy Nolan
Urbandale

THE CONTEST

It has been 383 days
since I've written a word or a phrase
that hasn't been part
of a shopping list or email.
The pen and my hand are negative
ends of magnets,
and still I wonder why it is
so excruciating to try to write?
Why would I rather pre-treat the stains
and clean out the closets?
I have recycled all my ideas
and have submitted everything
I have ever written already.
I am left with blank paper
and a hollow head.
The deadline is lurking
as I limp toward the finish line.
I could take all twenty lines you give me
and still want more
and still feel that I've said nothing.

Mary L Permann
Grimes

WAITING FOR WORD

It may be, I sadly fear
No published poem for me this year.
No news from the mail as summer passed by,
At least I'd given my very best try.

Then an envelope arrived addressed to me
My own handwriting it was plain to see.
Upon opening I read with joy and pride
One of my poems had indeed qualified!

Jan Logan
Van Horne

bartered nourishment

said this poet to that poet
   we could trade our words
      like good bread for sweet water

nothing fancy
   just enough to feed this poet's hunger
      and slake that poet's thirst

Beverly Mattix Green
Murray

IF THIS PAGE WERE TO BECOME A POEM

This page could be a lake
languid and reflecting the sun,
languishing in a breeze's soft song.
It could be a turkey
slipping out of the forest's grasp
and standing on the road for a moment,
leaving me to wonder
if it's real or a dream.
It could be a conversation
with an artist or a nurse
or the warm feeling that comes
before the words
and lingering after she's gone.
It could be a river,
desires ever-flowing
but never spent.
It could be an ocean
its waters touching the sky,
a pool of feelings
stirring inside me.

Mike Bayles
Davenport

THINGS TO DO AT A POETRY WORKSHOP
(in The Forestry Center)

Think.   Talk.   Eat.   Retreat
    seek relief for self

Make your bed   enjoy campfires
Hunt for glasses, stuff and words
Walk in woods and trail the pack
Fill sketchbook with potent images
    circle back to catered food
        eat camp fare

Walk to musty, dim-lit, cozy warmth
    of log house rooms
Find discovery under each porch
    stare back at raccoon

Watch the dry-land beach of rain-arranged duff,
Dodge mosquitoes
    search for Deet and swatters

Keep awake, inner systems wired

Thought without thought
Words without order ordered
Sense, sensibility and censors joined

Shirley Wyrick
Iowa City

NINETY YEARS OF CREATING CLUTTER

If you come with me to my dining room table
you'll see clutter, creative clutter…
papers, articles, books,
books everywhere.
The world awaits in a book.

Also, a portable sewing machine sits there.
I make quilts and tote bags to give away,
and there is a pile of grandsons' pants to patch.
Creative clutter.

Yet, Billy Collins, in one of his poems,
tells me, that he need spotlessness to be creative.
"Spotlessness is the niece of inspiration."
Not to me, Billy, clutter is king.
For, if I had had spotlessness,
I would have spent my whole life chasing dust.

Lila L Andersen
Independence

JUST ME

Hot & Sexy

Rent pd.

Tears topped,
missed, a bound
of words, then I
got to find — Heaven.

To have a few books
of a new world of one
though there were few,
like the heat of a
chase looking through

a cheetah. First on
a prairie that puts each
word up for rent where
we met with yes or
with answers.

To hear of where he
was or not!

Theresa Durkin
Des Moines

SNOWY KNIGHT

Maid a boll of popped corn.
Watching blizzard being born.
Cold, dark winter knight.
Full moon shining wight.
Dears feeding on bird cede;
Reel grate food knead.
Spring come! I'm forlorn.
Weighting for sonny mourn.
A picture of tee on trays.
Mi inn bleu pea jays.
Hear the steal kettle.
Under binkie I settle.
Know thing can beet
Warm tows and feat.

Carole L Pannhoff
Mason City

PULLING UP THE STAKES

Returning to the spot of the Big Top
Appears like crop circles of a strange origin…
Dusty flattened grass, popcorn boxes, peanut shells
And animal dung…
Trampled by beast and happy children
Lie on the ground.
The stapled circus flyer on a pole
Is my carefully removed keepsake.
Barnum and Bailey…
The circus has left town.
"The Greatest Show on Earth"
Out of step and time…
Only our memories behold you…
Gone forever.

Les McCargar
Gilman

MOVING ON

Four eagles in the river birch
out our kitchen window, their white
chests as wide as bedsheets, are so
patient. Only their heads move.

They remain still as pallbearers
awaiting the minister's nod.
We can't look away, don't
want to miss the grand lift-off.

But we must get back to
making the bed, fixing oatmeal,
checking our email. We miss
the flight, stare out at the bare birch.

John J Bowman
Iowa City

JASON

Walking in the river, in shoes, clothes and astonishment,
feeling there is no time but NOW, the clouds, the blueness of air,
and pearly white shells, the mussels river otters tasted,
smoothly we rainbow this wet beach

Catherine Dix Bonham
Aurelia

A BARRED OWL AT NIGHT

She screeches at the languid
moon, "Who cooks for you?"
Owl eats hares, shrews, rats…not baked,
stewed, or barbecued.
Her lonely question
echoes in the broth-thin light
of winter's crescent.

Shelly Jones Clark
Johnston

FLIGHT OF FANCY

A flock of geese were flying East to visit Martha's Vineyard.
They flew a line the crows defined, tacking slightly windward.

But then a breeze, a Southern wheeze made their leader tipsy.
Still on course, they were forced to land in North Poughkeepsie.

On Morgan Lake they met a drake who rode a fast Nor'easter.
He didn't mind the record time, just the cold wind on his keister.

"I'm not a doc," he told the flock, "But your leader has the vapors.
That South wind's damp and gives you cramps right where your torso tapers."

They took a break, the geese, the drake, to share their flying ventures.
The duck recalled a sight he saw that made him lose his dentures.

"Near Swan Boat Pond in Boston Town, Ma Duck and her ducklings
Bright as brass cross the grass ... and here's what makes my heart sing.

It's a statue of my great, great, great, great, great, great, great grandma.
And close behind you can find my great, great, great, great, great, great
        grandpa."

The geese agreed it was, indeed, a story without equal.
But they had to go, before, you know, the drake might start a sequel.

So off they flew to someplace new where ducks and swans are honored.
It's quite a find when you're inclined to visit Martha's Vineyard.

Larry Schroeder
Iowa City

THIRD GRADE CHOIR

Thirty bright-eyed songbirds
Perch on portable bleachers,
Heads bobbing, searching for parents,
As the director waves her hands skyward.

They peek over the wings
Of their open songbooks,
Mouths all O's, eagerly devouring
Scattered morsels of applause.

Warbling, chirping through the strains
Of "God Bless America,"
They fidget and flutter along imperfect rows--
The pianist's fingers flying to keep pace.

The choir exits in a cattywampus "V,"
But the flock soon abandons formation,
Hungry tummies leading them forward
Toward the noisy nest of the lunchroom.

William Dall
Dubuque

TEACHING MY GRANDSON HOW TO STEAL

We hug the large blue, mixing bowl as
Brody moves in close to watch the action.

Cracking eggs, stirring in flour and all of the rest
of the ingredients until it is a lumpy mixture
awaiting chocolate chips.

I sneak a bit of the cookie dough as his
big eyes dance at the thievery.
His small fingers dig in for his first bite of satisfaction.

A smile dances across his eyes as he dives in for a second bite.
Knowing this is a secret best kept with only his grandma.

Teresa Lawler
Ankeny

SPRING BREAK

Warm white sand filters between my toes,
Thundering waves refresh the canvas of the shore,
Reflections of the sun dance on their crests,
Again, again, again.

Jill Zimmerman
De Witt

RUBBER DUCKIES,

you have been in my camping life since she left you,
forsaken, a teeny-bopper who had to have you, couldn't live
without you, then parked you, inside our back door, alone,
to feel discarded, no longer needed.
Since I found you there, I have loved you,
made you mine, rubber duckies, even though…
                                        you'd been with another.
Each trek from camper to shower house, you carry dry toesies
across wet grass, protect feet from morning moistness,
wait patiently while I slip into your cousins, my flowery flip-flops,
let my body soak in an invigorating steamy shower,
then you carry me—toweled and lavender-lotioned—
back to our cozy little camper where hot
coffee, warm orange muffins, and he
waits for me
to step inside,
wearing you.
Rubber duckies, you're the ones, and I'm awfully fond of you.

*In 1985 'rubber duckies' were a rubber slip-on deck shoe which fashion-conscious teenage girls thought were just as cool as men's cotton boxers.

                                                          Margaret Westvold
                                                                          Ames

JULY RAIN

Blue rain pelts the pavement
like a drummer beating
on weary workers winding their way home.

Disappointed children peer
from porches, pounding fists
into stiff baseball mitts.

Sunflowers hunch over
heads cradling seeds
dropping petals into the mud.

Only earthworms surface
slinking along the sidewalks
gorging happily on succulent hosta leaves.

                                                                      Lynn Cavanagh
                                                                           Grinnell

the feast

when gathered to feast
don't fill up on sweet bread
let the yeast rise
it's a changing of the tide
a transformation of the whether inside
the carny professor is handing out
full rides to whoever cuts in line
don't worry the others won't mind
do fret,
a hundred grand in debt is just the first step
all that thinking will go straight to your head

Zachary Taylor Knox
Fort Madison

RED SEVEN BLUES

I lost it all a thousand times
and won it back again
One last race or hand of cards,
one more lucky spin

A dealer has no heart
a slot machine no soul
They will take it all, my friend,
and leave you in the cold

I'm trapped in a hell I made myself
and still I can not quit
Throwing down the last few dollars
because I'm just about to hit

I'm broke and I'm hungry
Got those Red Seven blues
A gambler has one kind of luck
Even when I win I lose

Jean Kitzmiller
Des Moines

JUDO

At first you complained about what we having for supper
I said nothing
Then you complained that we the same thing every Wednesday
I said nothing
You the food was cold
I said nothing
Then you ate it
I said nothing

Mike Fladien
Muscatine

HOME-SICK

Please keep driving straight dear.
Please don't take that turn.
I don't know where I want to go,
Just not home.

I'm tired of those empty walls,
Filled with noise that is masked.
Covering the air in its silent poise.
In the pain of the good ol' days.

Is there an opposite of homesick?
Being sick of home?
I'm not sure what going straight means for us,
I just don't want to go home yet.

Sometimes you get strangled by a blanket,
And sometimes warm is just too hot.
I love those lovely yellow walls,
I just don't want to go home yet.

We don't have to talk,
Or we can if you want to,
I just know.
I don't want to go home yet.

Reagan Mann
West Des Moines

MUSIC BOXED

Arthritic fingers unfastened the lid
watched intently as the ballerina
spun merrily, content to be dancing
In her younger years
she loved that tiny dancer
had listened happily to the tinkling tune
found joy and hope in every twirl
She pondered how life had changed her perception
she no longer saw a twirling beauty
free to dance and pirouette through life
She saw a plastic woman
spinning round and round
to the same tiring tune
trapped in a boxed life
never to be free
She slammed the lid shut

Marjorie Dohlman
Riceville

ONE-TWO-THREE

It began as a waltz
One-two-three, one-two-three
Just follow the steps you are given
Count: One-two-three, one-two-three
The dance started slow
The rhythm was easy
But, my partner is new
Doesn't count: one-two-three
Quickly the tempo increases
There's little time to breathe
The music is a frenzy
The notes are off key
When the final cord is played
The dance will be over
I have danced with the cancer
One-two-three, one-two-three.

LaVonne Augustson
Elkader

CONCERTS

I don't always listen to music on the radio,
But when there is a concert, I like to go.
The music is fine if it's rock, country or rap,
But if it's classical, I'll take a nap.
People at concerts sometimes like to dance,
But with two left feet, I don't take the chance.
My wife likes to line dance with some of her friends,
But do they ask me? It all depends.
Someone has to guard the purses and table,
I usually volunteer, if I am able.
I like to listen to the music, and maybe have a drink.
It's not pretty when I dance, I don't think.
So take me to a concert, and set me in a seat,
I'll enjoy the music, and quietly tap my feet.

Roger Brockshus
Spirit Lake

WINDCHIMES

tinkle lightly
clatter gaily
crash wildly
bump intermittently
hang silently

Ginnie Padden
Des Moines

A PENTECOSTAL EXPLAINS HIS ENTHUSIASM

God is a ways away
Jesus has a body
The Spirit is diffuse
All the saints are bloody

Shout to be heard by God
Agonize with a saint
Speak to Christ as other
Into the Spirit faint

God is too far yonder
Christ corpus too concrete
The saints too medieval
But the Spirit is sweet

Laura Felleman
Iowa City

FOR A MOMENT

A paper mâché Jesus
In a toothpick crib
Popsicle sticks, Mary and Joseph,
Dressed in colored ribbon
Soda straw shepherds, popcorn sheep
Pipe cleaner wise men, cardboard camels
White napkin angel with silver sparkles
A tinfoil star lights up Bethlehem

For a moment
The world shines
When we make believe

Richard K Wallarab
Coralville

SHINY PEOPLE

I've lost interest in the shiny people
With their untarnished lives and varnished image.
I used to try to be shiny.
But now, mostly, I don't care.
I want to be with people whose shine has been rubbed off,
Who've let life crack them open
So I can actually see inside.
And be with what is real.

Mary Clover
Marshalltown

COCKTAIL PARTY

Look--
    how the group moves
        amoeba-like
            through the room
      not knowing
    where it wants to go,
        connected to itself
           by transparent threads
      that suddenly break off,
    forming a new group
      that starts its life
closer to the bar.

Linda E Paul
North Liberty

WORLD DESOLATION

Yes, old woman, I've been told about you
You were once young such a beautiful whim
Dressed in your seductive shimmering blue

Many charming admirers you drew
Did not you have a special secret him?
Yes, old woman, I've been told about you

Were you rejected to be bid adieu?
Surprisingly, you were sawed from the limb
Dressed in your seductive shimmering blue

Your skin was fresh as the morning dew
And grace filled your perfection to the brim
Yes, old woman, I've been told about you

Almighty God's glory filled you anew
Your heart outpoured praise with vigor and vim
Dressed in your seductive shimmering blue

Your true love for Him you chose to pursue
As your worldly values grew quite dim
Desolate woman, I've been told about you
Dressed in your seductive shimmering blue

Beverly Boal
Des Moines

COMPUTER PASSWORDS

Bravo Alpha Bravo, Charlie Charlie,
Foxtrot Alpha Romeo, Papa Bravo,
Tango India, Papa Foxtrot,
Echo Delta, Echo Sierra, Echo Alpha,
Hotel Tango, Whiskey Romeo.

John Mitchell
West Des Moines

SAY HELLO TO ARTIE

Will fill in your blanks, take care of your sins.
Drive your SUV, track your gaming wins.
Will clean your carpets, and mow your lawns.
Monitor your perimeter from dusk until dawn.

I am here to perform all your menial tasks,
plan your menus and fill your glasses.
Locate the best online website to use,
sign up for hot dates, find one to peruse.

The age of Artificial Intelligence is here,
in some ways smart, but you need not fear:
"IT" can do single tasks well, that is clear,
but not feel, plan or love, or know what is dear.

Some workers will have to find new occupations,
Yet society will be freed from common frustrations.
Already my email spells and greets friends for me;
When IT composes my holiday greetings, then I'll feel glee.

Mike Wilson
Des Moines

MY DAILY STRUGGLE

ADD 1, 2…
Oh, were you talking to me?
I really don't know how
The remote to the TV
Ended up in the freezer.
I didn't do it either!
Oh, wait
I ate something a little bit ago
But how that remote got there,
I don't know.

Brianna Carter
Cedar Falls

ENTRY

"The home seems pleasant.
Your roommate is jolly."
(And, thank God, she has her mind!)
"You'll like it here, I know.
Well, I have to go.
I'll see you often."
I escape
only to pass a shape in a wheelchair
with eyes glazed like taxidermy art,
a trophy of modern medicine.
A cry off in another wing
quickens my pace down a too-long hall.
I lunge into the out-of-doors
shaking institution from me.
In the rush of days that follow
you are often on my mind,
but I put your new address
in my book in pencil.

Kathryn Jons Roelfsema
Iowa Falls

FADING AWAY

Beatrice, Nebraska...
My two-year-old grandson, awaiting my visit, runs to the front door each time a car zips down his street. When I arrive, words tumble from his mouth like poured cereal. He excitedly shows me his sing-along videos, brings me books to read, and invites me to hold his "yittle" brother. The next morning, he chatters enthusiastically as I take him for a ride in a jogging stroller.

Sheldahl, Iowa...
My eighty-four-year-old father-in-law, anticipating my arrival, stares out his kitchen window and counts cars on a back road that eventually leads me to him. Although specific words often fail him, he offers me cookies and tries to sweeten my milk with orange juice. His brilliant mind and weathered hands work jigsaw puzzles with my wife while FOX News blares across the living room from the TV set. The reception I get in these border states feels eerily similar, but only my grandson can remember my name.

Stephen E Leach
Huxley

JEWELS

She called them jewels—
Her jars of food,
Beans, beets, and peaches
Tomatoes red, corn of gold.
Shelf after shelf,
Gleaming there.
The fruits of her labor
Jewels beyond compare.
Summer was over
Cold and snow instead;
Contentment and believing
Her family will be fed.

Marjorie Moore
Indianola

FAMILY REUNION

Coming together with smiles big and wide,
old grudges forgotten or just set aside.

We eat and we talk about those who've departed.
Yes, wild Uncle George had our Grandma outsmarted.
Who in the past was a saint, who a sinner:
Not one of our bunch can stand out as a winner.
Some topics I hope we will fail to discuss.
We all know the ones that will cause a big fuss.

Politics clearly is what to avoid.
Aunt Polly's a Democrat; says so with pride.
Great Uncle Bill, who's as prideful as she,
says Republican virtues have kept our land free.
The squabbles go on for a day and a night.
All debaters are sure only their points are right.

Aunt Betsy serves food. Every bit is delicious,
but cranky old Fred starts in acting suspicious
of his brother Ted who responds with loud laughter,
which really was not what old Freddie was after.
So Aunt Betsy goes up and says into Fred's ear,
"This party is over. We'll see you next year."

Ethel Barker
Iowa City

FIRST SNOWFALL DIRTY DANCING

She was a satin gowned wisp that fell from the sky
He rose up from the road when a pickup drove by
Swirling around clumsy, mud caked hoofed cattle
Launching off the barn door, making it rattle
Twirling atop the hen house, gliding over eaves
Light-footed barnyard merriment stirring up leaves
Alas, a whirlwind romance destined not to survive
For the briefest of moments, a love theme revived
She now blankets the branches of a coniferous fir
He lies masking a slippery patch, a silent saboteur
With no regrets for their duets in an unruly fashion
Each blast of wind reignites their unbridled passion

Jill Lockey
Janesville

GLENN GOULD PLAYS CONCERTO NUMBER 5, LARGO *(Bach)*

Languid sounds permeate
Slithering into my soul
Lingering
Soothing
Helixing forward
Heart pulsating
Blood circulating
Alive
Vital
Asulta

Last movement

Crescendo
Reality
Presto.

Norbe Birosel Boettcher
Marion

SIDEWALK WALTZ

Scoop-two-three, lift
then throw snow to the right,
scoop-two-three, lift
then throw snow to the right.

Pivot with shovel a quarter turn left
then scoop-two-three straight ahead,
shuffle left,
scoop-two-three straight ahead,
one square of sidewalk is clear.

Step-two-three next square
then forty-eight more.

Joe Chambers
Davenport

TWENTY-EIGHT FALLS

I've been raking leaves at my place
now for twenty-eight Falls.
After all these years, I'm finding it
to be a real pain in the – neck.

But what the heck. I don't mow
much in the summer, but come
autumn it's a bummer.

So I rake and I burn and I use the
leaf blower. But every Fall I'm older
and a little bit slower.

I have many new neighbors with
many young kids to be found. I
should employ some of them and
sit around. And watch football.

Twenty-eight Falls I've been raking
leaves. Twenty-eight Falls.

I'm ready to call it a career and
be done. Then someone else can
have the fun.

Pat Hanson
North Liberty

AH, NOVEMBER!!!

November is for reaping what has been sown.
If January is a new babe, and March is a teen,
November must be where I am now, just stepping into 70.
Moses speaks of three score years and ten.

Leviticus earmarks a value in silver
For males between 20 and 60, as 50 shekels.
The value for those above 60 is reduced to 15 shekels.
Diminishing strength, diminishing value.

Really? A monetary value cannot be put on experience.
But there is one man Who lived over 2000 years ago
Whose death and resurrection
Gave value to babes with Trisomy 13 and 21.

Jesus did that for His children.
My strength may be diminishing, but NOT my value.
Up from here is Maranatha!
So welcome, November, the window into winter.

Mary Sue Moss
Dallas Center

THE PROBLEM

Had homework to do,
But first I wanted
To fix my problem,
So that it would
Be easier to concentrate.
I searched up
Ways to help me by:
Browsing through
The web,
Watching videos
On YouTube,
And asking friends
On social media.
Finally,
I decided to go
To bed because
It was getting late,
But at least I knew
How not to
Procrastinate.

Matthew Faulkner
Fort Madison

AM I THERE YET?

Hurry, hurry, rush and scurry—
Holidays are such a flurry!

Dust the house and clean those floors,
Put up the tree and decorate doors.

Bathe the dogs (now there's two),
Mail those cards; so much to do.

Clean the basement and comb that cat
(She's in there somewhere under matt).

Bake those goodies; is that too hard?
And start upon a Christmas card!

Get out the pretties and trim that tree,
Turn on the lights for friends to see.

And get out those cards before it's too late!
How do I handle this disordered state?

Call up our friends and say 'hello';
Load up that car so we're ready to go.

It's Christmas with family we're aiming for;
But first get those cards to the post office door.

Oh, me! Oh, my! My whirling head!
But, first things first—get out of bed!

Linda M Nash
Fort Madison

GOING WHERE?

A motor home,
the open road,
a tank full of gas,
destination unknown.

A camera in hand,
GPS in mode,
where shall we go?
stay or pass?

Angela Smith
Iowa City

the sentimental-septuagenarian

i have lost my directions
where is the big dipper

i never became a cowboy
joined the mickey mouse club
wore buster brown shoes

life has taken me full circle
eyes partially blind
ears nearly deaf
nostrils that can't smell
hair as thin as a newborn babe

attention span zero
memory locked into the past

i have turned into a slow-talkin'
slow-walkin' great-grandfather

graying with beloved granny
gravitating towards our 50th wedding anniversary

finding out
what all those who have gone before felt

….you'll have to find out for your self
    i will tell you no more….

michaelandorf
Brandon

RETIREMENT

Not the end, but just beginning a new phase that is all the rage; say my 60-something friends.

First day, slept all the way till 5:30 am; left lots of REM cycles un-gotten.

First week, tongue in cheek, thought I'd get more done; no plans, just errands run.

First month, started to relax. Worked my list to the max. Began positive, productive routines if you know what I mean…. like exercising three days per week, getting up at seven not eleven.

Planning stage is over, time to get sober and finish a project that's been in the closet; for so many years while the kids grew through their tears, got out of school, and learned The Golden Rule, moved out and on; "Oh the Places They'll See" without Dad and Me.

Oh, those projects…, makes so much logic to finish them now with the know-how and the money (isn't it funny?) how there seems to be more in our bank's store. Hobbies expanded now that we've landed into a routine; writing, crafting, photography, traveling, and volunteering.

With the kids gone we can sing our own song of retirement, "We'll Do It Our Way" (until called back home to babysit the grandkids of course!)

Audrey Mueller
De Witt

ASSISTED LIVING CHANT

Ding…dong…ding…dong…dinner bell's…noon song…
Doors…slam…wham…bam…hinges…squeak…creatures…speak…
We…are…old…we…are…slow…we…need…help…don't…you…know?

Wheelchairs…roll…walkers…stroll…carts…click…canes…tick…
Shoes…slap…flippers…flap…boots…stop…sneakers…clop…
We…are…old…we…are…slow…we…need…help…don't…you…know?

Where's…my table…where's…my chair…can't remember…here or there
Those green beans…we…won't…take…give us…lobster…give us…steak
We…are…old…we…are…slow…we…need…help…don't…you…know?

We've…been…fed…now…to…bed…we…need…rest…lost…our…zest…
Here's…my…room…one-o-one…close…the…drapes…too…much…sun
We…are…old…we…are…slow…we…need…help…don't…you…know?

We…feel…ill…need…some…pills…life…line…sounds…
Nurse…makes…rounds…they…come…quick…when…you…are…sick…
We…are…old…we…are…slow…we…need…help…don't…you…know?

Dixie Kanago
Spencer

ODE TO AN AGING STAR

She greets her loyal fans daily, bundled with excitement.
As her band loosens, she takes her place,
not at the head of the table, but on top of it--
demanding space and attention.
She is always a guest of honor, always a welcome visitor;
admirers casually digest every word she utters.

She recalls being the "it" girl; for decades she held that title.
Subscribers eagerly awaited her headlines,
Black ink declaratively covered events of the world.
People clamored for her extra editions,
admiring her timely accuracy and in-depth analysis.
She created a love affair with both politics and pop culture.

She's not as thick as in her younger days,
days filled with international headlines and local events.
Frail in her old age, she shrinks from the competition.
The glamorous alternatives are high tech and edgy--
online headlines feed on fake news and fancy algorithms.
Truth, lost in her dwindling pages, costs more yet delivers less.
Some call it supply and demand; others call her old fashioned.
In time, all will refer to her as history.

Kelcy Lofgren
Ankeny

THE OUTTHERE

    we inhale oxygen,

    along with the OutThere that sustains us,

    as our heart pumps a few beats closer

    toward the time rhythm is spent,

    and when we, ourselves,

    become the OutThere

    our ancestors will breathe in.

Tim Grover
Pleasant Hill

WELL BEING

Yesterday you were screaming
today you are laughing
you must feel better!
No—I am still
screaming.
You just can't hear me.

Barbara Brooks Wheeler
Cedar Falls

LET'S TALK IT OVER

Past noon, and while two cats ate
   breakfast, I've yet to fix anything
I'll continue to chew with front teeth
   though nothing to chew, liquids only

I'm on a liquid diet after extractions
   took three out leaving 29 or so
I may die toothless but I'm hoping
   for many more years semi teethed

Don't call me toothless, not yet
   I'll bare my teeth at the dentist
   the next time he says open wide
I'm not giving up easily, not next time

No teeth needed to chew on old times
   dreams that failed reality's rhythms
   loves that up and went, graveside
Life's bright visions sacrificed, buried

Bucket list tossed into moving waters
Youthful goals and fantasies adrift
   distress calls to no one, in darkness
Let's talk it over, embrace, speak low

Paul C Sabelka
West Union

LIFE THROUGH A STRAW

I often drink life through a straw.
From high pressure to low,
   flavors and textures adorn
   most things I need to know.
Were the mind likened to
  a carnivorous beast
  mine would insist on prime—
  well-marbled, dry aged
  and seared to perfection.
This I would gladly chew, but
  I would not forsake my straw,
  as it lends balance, most of all.
Meat juices flow and find
   their way to my brain,
   providing a reptilian pleasure
   beyond mere sustenance,
   a vivid carnival ride in reverse—
   clattering back to a primordial hiss.

Thomas Georgou
Coralville

ALCOHOL NUMBS

Alcohol numbs the pain hiding
Self-loathing and fear residing
In weeds that root and hold on tight
Pronouncing claim as earned birthright
Strength and weakness crash colliding

Evil whispers, hissing, chiding
Good intentions fall, slip, sliding
Firestorms again ignite
Alcohol numbs

Sobriety's strength subsiding
Reality fades while guiding
Only losers in bloodless fight
As drink and drinker reunite
Death unblinking its time biding
Alcohol numbs

Rebecca Whitmore
Muscatine

AN ADDICT'S PRAYER

Dear Jesus, save me from my destruction.
I can't do this all alone.
I want to walk with you every day
And to turn over a new stone.

This addiction is the darkness in my life.
The sun never shines through.
Help me learn the errors of my ways
So I may be more like you.

Grant me the strength to overcome this
And to be the person people used to know.
The happy, carefree woman with the heart of gold
And let the goodness flow.

Please, bless my family
They stood with me through it all.
Help me not to fail them.
Please, help me not to fall.

Angie Cochran
Argyle

PRIORITIES

    doggies   day care
    kitties   you tube stars
    babies   starving

Kathy Geren Christy
West Burlington

THE ONGOING STRUGGLE
(The Black Rights Matter Movement)

The orbs watch and wait
Hidden in the emerald green leaves
It waits for a mistake
We are resilient
And that makes it scared
We are black and powerful
Our strides strong
Our eyes sharp
We are black and beautiful
With a history filled with pain
With broken bones
Bruised backs
Wrung necks
And despite it all, every morning
As the whites of our eyes redden
Scrubbing off the words created to belittle us
We know, we are black and bulletproof
Any revolutionary praxis for change starts with us
It hides in behind the greens, afraid
We are unstoppable

Alyssa Ashmore
West Des Moines

A SHELTER AGAINST VIOLENCE
(After a visit to a women's protective shelter)

When you walk in the night,
All alone in your plight,
Amidst the darkness too thick to fight,
Remember somewhere there is light.

When the well overflows with your tears,
And your hopes dissolve into fears,
Amidst a time where truth is no longer right,
Remember somewhere there is light.

When your pain from hate filled blows
Overtakes your body and constantly grows;
When your fatigue reaches a new height,
Remember somewhere there is light.

When even your children are in danger,
And the predator is not a stranger,
While your arms hold them all tight,
Remember somewhere there is light.

Nancy Peters
Sheldon

THE CONE

Every man wears The Cone
Fastened around his neck
Interferes with The Mask
Keeps him from licking the private
Where he was licked by
A Cone wearer long ago
It keeps a man clean
Who has never been seen
The Cone and the Mask
Are up to the task
Some will wear off
Before they tear off
Sandusky taught us abruptly
Cone wearers come from places high and low
Money, status quo and "Me Too"
The Wounded Healer came by one day
Took off my Cone and threw it away

Bill Perry
Ottumwa

PEACE ON EARTH
Advent 2018

In the second year of the presidency of Donald Trump,
    when Kim Reynolds was governor of Iowa,
and Vladimir Putin was president of Russia,
    and Xi Jinping was president of China,
and Netanyahu was prime minister of Israel,
    during the time of Francis as Pope,
the word of God came to Carol
    to proclaim throughout the news media:

"Awake. Everyone. Quiet the chaos of your minds.
    Triumph over every evil action -- without exception.
Watch. Countries shall lay down arms.
    Every hater and maligner shall surrender.
All bombs shall be silenced.
    Demons shall be defenseless.
Then all people shall see the baby-soft skin of our Savior."

Carol Sisterman
St Ansgar

POINT AWAY

Long before last spring
As high school sweethearts
You taught me how to aim your .22
At rusted cans dappling quarry rubble.

On squirrel hunts
Cross barbed fences and fallen trees,
You'd repeat "Point gun to ground, keep safety on. Always."
Till you knew I'd never forget.

After high school left woods and you behind.
Jarred back by classmate's call
Foreclosure divorce depression
Found by a tent
You and your gun
At wood's edge.

Private burial. No flowers. A sudden death.
Thin paper words shroud the truth—
Barbed fears cut too deep to cross.

Back in autumn woods
Crisp crunch walk towards a rusty pasture fence,
I recite your words never to forget.

Adrienne Coffeen
Decorah

DIRTY LAUNDRY

Once in a while,

I air my dirty laundry.

It smells better, but

I know it's not fresh.

To really clean it,

I must wash it in

the scalding water

of truth,

scour it on the wash board

of redemption,

liberally applying the detergent

of repentance.

Kass Harper
Cedar Falls

THE WALL

I saw The Wall at Nogales,
and at Agua Prieta, and Naco:
an ugly tall iron snake that purports
to separate Mexico from the United States.
It is a monument to American arrogance
and futility, since it can be climbed over
or scrambled through with the help
of giant shears and acetylene torches.
It is the altar upon which American infrastructure,
arts, and humanities will be sacrificed
since U.S. citizens, not Mexicans,
will pay for this barbaric structure.
I have walked along the Great Wall of China,
a much more ambitious undertaking.
That wall failed, as will the American one.

David M Gradwohl
Ames

EROSION

Little pieces fall off of me
Bits of broken dreams
And old memories
My cells scream
As the detritus
Separates us

Paul Durdan
Camanche

CHANGING TIMES

"Volunteers! Where are all my volunteers?"
The distraught preacher asks, in tears,
"Who donates the funereal cakes and pies?"
He moans and wipes streaming eyes.

"And what of do-good women's clubs?
No one takes office or even subs.
No one works for free, not chili dippers,
Youth leaders, nor pancake flippers."

"Not me!" the female chorus sings from work.
"We've no time for kinder, nor for kirche.
We're doctors, dentists, and leaders, too,
Hundreds of important jobs we now do."

Myrna Sandvik
Brandon

AFTER SUNRISE

When broken sunlight saunters
across the crazy
quilt of Montana's
jagged horizon

When I awaken once more
to smell dew-soaked pines
hear songbird greetings
over whispering streams

When I watch for the last time
gray shadows transform
to shades of pink-red
fading to sky blue

Then I'll be content to rest
eyes closed forever
silent and at peace
right after sunrise

Maxine Carlson
Iowa City

MY SANCTUARY

A day in blissful solitude
    In nature's rustic home
Amid the untamed wilderness
    Secluded but not alone

The whisper of a gentle breeze
    Flutters through the trees
Birds sing in harmony
    Nature's symphony

The bubbling of a winding brook
    Running wild and free
Laughing as it overflows
    Destination a mystery

Footprints on a beaten path
    Lead to the unknown
Uninvited company
    Forsaken and forlorn

In the stillness of creation
    Echoes the Spirit's song
A touch of Heaven's glory
    A place where I belong

Terry Overocker
Milford

THE PEACEFUL PLACE

There's a house far from town,
and a lane you go down,
that's far from the noise of the city.
It's where the squirrels play,
on a crisp autumn day,
and to scare them would be such a pity.
They go up and down trees,
they hide, then they seek,
forever running to and fro.
It's quite a peaceful place
this home with rare grace,
where the wind says, "please don't go,"
where the world stays away,
for yet another day,
and the wind says, "please don't go."

Esther Marlene Gardner
Melrose

AS EVENING TURNS TO NIGHT IN THE PARK

My battery is low and it's getting dark,
Ending this evening in the park.
I often come here by this landmark,
Searching for that one, creative spark.

Today didn't work out though,
Couldn't find the right word just so.
With my battery getting low,
It will soon be time to go.

I like writing on this laptop,
It was pretty cheap at the pawnshop.
But now it is getting time to stop,
In fact I think I feel a raindrop.

So considering the battery and the weather,
I don't want to ruin this jacket leather.
Maybe tomorrow something will come together,
But right now it's time to go home to Heather.

I know when returning to the carpark,
I'll hear that familiar and friendly skylark.
He always bids me with a remark,
As evening turns to night in the park.

Brad Hesford
Muscatine

A FULL AND BRIGHT MOON

Last night I gazed upon the full and bright moon,
   reminding me of summer nights growing up in a small town.
How fireflies used to dance above the ground
   on long walks with my love, and the moon
   would reflect in his soft eyes.
Far away from ones I held dear in my heart,
   distance was shortened knowing they too were gazing
   upon the same moon.
Even now, I wonder if we share the same sight,
   if the gap between us is not less because we share
   the same full and bright moon.

Lynn Kramer
Iowa Falls

STAR CHILD

as I regard the vaulted night sky I clearly
see myself. a reflection of stardust that
      has traveled across boundless
      eons of space and time
from ancient, uncharted worlds.
I am a drop of primordial ooze,
      and the dark loamy sand
         of centuries yet to be
…a tiny glimmer of existence in the endless
   ever changing universe.
never the less I am a child of creation,
temporal and self-evident, glistening
         shining with life.
my appointed destiny, though hidden, is only
waiting to be realized. discovered within the
continuing reality of the ever unfolding now.

Rick Sears
Mason City

ADORATION OF LUNA

face of the moon,
rapturous cratered wink.
full prowess witnessed, in cycling weeks

ocean's tides swoon,
halted beasts chorus hymns.
furless monkeys impart, fire metal ships

celestial light,
vague guide to heaven's stars.
Sol's envious gaze, blazes afar

Terra glows bright,
yet forgets your dear gift.
for seditious moments, solar eclipse

Nathan Kolacia
Iowa City

TO THE NEW YEAR

You are the apprentice
I have been waiting for.
I can teach you the song
from which all singing emerges.

The doors of ecstasy
could then open.

You could be different
from those others.

Transparent, like the sunlight
that gives so much
we have no more capacity
for wonder.

Suzanne Araas Vesely
Fairfield

STILLNESS

The stillness of the house
meanders like a lost kitten
with soft and silent feet.

The clicking of a clock,
the clunking of the ice maker,
the whirring of the fan

the only sounds disturbing the peace.
The darkness covers the sound like
a soft cloth.

Soon the early birds will add
their sounds along with
the frantic frogs' vocals.

The quiet disappears with the darkness,
the noisy day begins with dawn's arrival
and the sun's rising.

Goodbye stillness,
old friend, hello new day,
new friend.

Rita F Reed
Waukee

SUMMER SOUNDS

Hear the cardinals singing in the tree,
    Squirrels chattering as they feed.
The loud crack of a baseball bat,
    And the sound of a fly swatter, Splat!
Fans produce a continuous drone;
    Lawn mowers whirl as grass is mown.
Relaxing in the summer shade;
    Hear crackling ice in a glass of lemonade.
Excited voices from children at play;
    A church bell chime at the end of the day.
Booming thunder wakes the town
    As summer rain comes pelting down.

Mary Peterson
Rock Rapids

DO YOU HEAR

Do you hear the sound
calling in the still morn?
Do you feel the crisp, cold air
as the mournful tune is played
and feel the shivers travel
down your back?
Now do you hear my dog
waking all who sleep
as he barks and howls
yes, at that silly freight train
traveling through our town!

Karen Carr
Mason City

A NOISY NEIGHBOR

My neighbor has a hot rod car.
You know how they are,
Va-room, Va-room,
Always up early for his work or play,
But I'm not ready to start my day.
At night, the story is still the same.
I know his little game,
Told his mother this has gone too far.
Said she'd try to talk to him,
I'm quite sure she never did.
I faced Fred with awful dread.
You've got to stop that racket.
Guess what Freddie said, "VA-ROOM!"
I'm on my way to city hall,
An official order will settle all.
"Freddie, all I have to say,
I'm glad that va-room has gone away."

Lucy Ringold
Des Moines

NO FEAR

Silence broken, enchanting and eerie,
strong, solid and bold, not weak or weary.
The call "Yip, Yip, Howooo" sings exultantly,
the crowning final note ebbs elegantly,
as the wail echoes deep into the west
announcing from the hills' encircling crest:
"I am Coyote and I am here!"

Bill Haywood
Janesville

THE MIGHTY UNTAMED

She bubbles up to trickle
Picks up steam
Like the ancient vessels that churned her.
Beating, assaulting, pushing against her power
To use as their own.
Wider now at points south
Rushing to a silted sea of constant return
Pulling life with her above and below.
These humans try to harness her
Cover her rapids, erect dams and walls
Keep her out of their basements, off lawns
And concrete ribbons they use for foot and wheel transport.
Yet she rises.
Overtakes their creations.
Floods their ingenuity
Has her way.
Roils, writhes, flows, recycles and
Begins again
With bubbles and a trickle at the top of Lake Itaska.

Teresa LaBella
Davenport

PEBBLES

Shiny pebbles on the beach
Sharp edges now refined
Tumbled in the crashing waves
Shaped slowly over time

Ironically, those ugly stones
Harshly treated at surf's hand
Transform to polished beauties
Showcased upon the sand

Michelle Turner
Maquoketa

PLATTE* **

Just an old stream like many others showing its age in
    countless curves meandering though the flatland.
But it is rendered in gold and, indeed, there is something
    priceless about the scene.
Even the oxbow in the foreground is emphatic and extra-
    leisurely as it winds along.
I'll bet there are morel mushrooms growing there in
    springtime—
John would know just where to look, I imagine.
It flows slowly across the corner of one state and into
    the next—
Where cranes fly by under golden clouds, and soak their
    long legs in its goldish flow.

* or "fly-way"
** about a painting hanging in the 200 Sun Room, North Mahaska Care Facility

Rob Hoskinson
Oskaloosa

THE JOY IN IOWA

Oh there is pollen in the air,
And the smell of manure,
There is no compare.

The beautiful green fields,
    They turn brown.
And get stuck behind a farmer
hauling his harvest to town!

The wind she does blow!
    You may even ask
Where did my lawn furniture go!

Those no-see-em bugs,
    Those son-of-a-guns,
They give you a bite that will make you forget
    You were having fun!

There are cold winter nights,
And the heat on those hot summer days!
    Lucky for us, that's when we make hay.

Just a few of the things that bring us joy.
Living in Iowa, sometimes all you can say is,
    Oh boy!

Susan Ferry Osland
Manilla

WINTER IN IOWA

Sparkling flakes of new fallen snow
Accompanied by the cold winds that blow.
Trees naked grasping so very tight
To frost collected in the winter's night.
Blades of grass which were once green
Covered now in a reflective white sheen.
Snow threatened only by a warm sunny day
Replaces itself with more that will stay.
Colorful winter birds in tree branches teeter
Waiting for special treats of a bird feeder.
Squirrels with tails flicking across the ground
Playing joyfully without making a sound
Sounds of shovels and blowers echo in the air
Revealing muscles and joints in need of repair.
Noisy snow mobiles looking for snow now abound
While skis skip across hillsides of frozen ground.
Yes, winter is here once again, my friends,
Here in Iowa, like it or not, 'til spring begins.

Ron E Squires
Oelwein

OUR IOWA

A nourishing rain
Fell this morning;
A February thunderstorm
Came without warning.

The temperature rose
T'will be warm today.
It feels like Spring
Is well on its way.

This winter has left
Little snow or ice.
It made the season
Oh, so nice!

Living in Iowa
We rarely expect
What weather is next,
We learn to accept.

An Iowa quote
To end this poem:
You call it Heaven;
We call it Home.

Mary Louise Berhow
Ames

ODE TO DUST

Dust…universal contaminant
Lowly, unwanted, despised
Fine, gritty powder that defies a cloth
Swirls into corners, onto shelves, under beds

Dust…an invisible, invincible presence
Clogs pores
Grinds machinery to a halt
Makes dull all it touches

Dust…dirt by another name
Your malleable nature reveals your power
Hard, unyielding, strong
Yet soft, pliable, nourishing source of life

Dust…unjustly maligned
Your value is discernible only to an inner eye
A sense that sees beyond the obvious
From you comes the apex of creation…Man

Margaret Smolik
Osage

ODE TO MILKWEED

Aurora blue flowers
bordering abolished by herbicides
proudly prevail,

a roadside landing zone
for migrating butterflies;
silky nectar nourishes
the Monarch orbit,
a plenary path
indulgent in leaves;
caterpillars help themselves.

Diverse seeds avail man
affray plotting,
armor regeneration.

Joy Lyle
Keota

A GUESSING GAME

Take me back to how it was before,
Knowing I can't talk to you just makes me want more.
I messed it up, I know I did.
I tried to be nice,
tried to be what I thought was a good friend.
It doesn't matter now because it bit me in the end…
Are you gone for good or just for now?
I wish you'd tell me,
give me some peace somehow.
It's always a guessing game,
Was it me?
Am I to blame?
Or is this just…you?
Is this something you usually do?
I thought I knew you; maybe I'm wrong?
Maybe this poem is my sign to move on.

Madison Vos
Spirit Lake

SOMEONE TO HANG MY LOVE ON

Astrologically,
I had so much love
to give - which was whetted
by love song after love song,
by romance novel after romance novel,
into an emotion well formed.

I am afraid my frustration was no
person on which to hang the
love. I looked, made an
attempt on several men -
without much success.

My husband and I are
still married after
thirty-three years.
We love each other.
Mentally, I no longer
take seriously
that emotion my
insides had
formed. But…

Margot Conard
Stratford

THE TREE OF LOVE

If my wife were a tree, she would be a combination of the most beautiful and elegant trees in the rain forest. She would be the tallest and most impressive, rising proudly above the canopy, head thrust nobly towards the sun.

Her limbs would extend far and wide, embracing the life around her, giving shelter, purpose and special meaning to any animals that come within her sphere.

Her roots, extending below those tapered slabs, would plunge deeply into the red soil beneath her, and then sideways for vast lengths, anchoring her firmly as she draws her strength from the minerals and nutrients that cycle through her world paying homage to her majesty, exultant to soon share in her great destiny.

Sean McMahon
Cumming

THEY DANCED

They touched hands,
And life would never be the same.
Holding each other tight, eyes closed,
they danced.

Then life really happened,
new partners, families formed, babies born
and the years passed.
No time to dance.

Now each alone, they met again,
shared stories, showed pictures,
smiled and laughed.
The years vanished.

Life had come full circle.
Reaching out, hands holding tight
over the arms of their wheelchairs
their eyes closed, and they danced.

Jerry Roberts
Jefferson

SCENTS OF PINE

Welcome the light, peering eerily through the trees
As it gently welcomes the midnight breeze.
Making way through memories of branches,
foliage of folly, rays that arch past trenches.
Light finds a way, to trudge through forgotten leaves
Leaving a trail of fickle faith, as mind and fate interweave.
A bright green garment that you wore last
weaves through trees, a scent of pine, from the past.

Ali Arsanjani
Fairfield

LOSS

No funeral procession
Or room filled with mourners
No bereavement leave
Or respectful mourning period
Acknowledged by others

Where the obituary
Or neighborly food offerings
Where the sympathy
Or understanding of
Enormous loss

Why didn't the world stop
Why aren't flags half-staff
Why does the sun still shine
Why do birds still sing
Amidst such gloom

Adorned with fur
Kneading four paws into my heart
Tearing my soul with your claws
Rumbling purr
Silenced evermore

Andrea Dorn
Nevada

NOT A FUNERAL POEM

After the funeral,
unwritten poems chase each other in my head.
I want to grab them,
but they are elusive, just out of reach.

If only I could capture
the metaphor about the brevity of life,
then maybe I could convince myself
to make the most of the years I have left.
If I could somehow tackle
the theme about the importance of family,
perhaps it would force me
to appreciate my family more.
And if I could brush up against
the simile about surviving grief,
perhaps I could secure it on paper
before it scatters.

All I know is my thoughts
are as broken as my heart.
None of this is salvageable
without you.

Erin Cavanagh
Wellman

HE WOULD HAVE—

—left cultivating his precious corn rows
to push my wheelchair
through the maze of clinic halls

—foregone his favorite Gunsmoke episode
to tuck another blanket around my chilled body
put a heated pad on my cold feet

—counted out the daily pills
driven twenty miles to bring almond chicken
when nothing else tasted good

—given up morning coffee with friends
to bless my face with warm, wet cloths
prayed for my comfort and healing

—tired of my need but kissed away the tears
and finally called our children to my bedside

—he would have done all this
if he had not gone first

Joan Jessen Waske
Afton

I GUESS I'M STILL IN MOURNING

Today I discarded his toothbrush
It's been seven years since he went to heaven
I just couldn't do it before
But it is time, since some healing has been given

I am sorrowful of numerous earthly things
That have happened to my friends and me
But I take comfort that I have never been alone
Because God oversees what is to be

I long for heaven myself sometimes
It's a tough world going along
And then I take another thankful breath
And know, now, this is where I belong

I'm trying to build up my strength again
And the "blue meanies" will soon go away
So now I need to remember I'm loved
And may I deserve that honor, I pray.

Judy A Gustafson
Rock Rapids

TAPS

Five older men sit in the corner playing cards, spinning tales, wearing their American Legion hats, rifles rest in the corner. The American flag has been rolled and put back in its case again. "I never get used to this funeral thing," says one of the men, "he was such a good guy, still had stories to tell, I choke up when I hear taps."

As they sit and reminisce, tales float over the group, about this invasion and that battle, their wives and sweethearts, loneliness and the sergeant they couldn't stand. How they can never talk about this "stuff" with their families, they wouldn't understand."

Will we ever see their kind again? Sharing with each other, common goals, getting things done and tending to their business. A country together, a united effort and a job well done. These men of the greatest generation want no credit and now spend their spare time honoring newly fallen comrades...as the final bugle sounds, still giving their all.

Margery L Watts
Stuart

THE OLD SOLDIER'S QUILT

My husband, a Korean War Vet
Did not have a memory quilt yet.
He's one of three brothers still alive,
Who experienced military life.
I decided it was about time
To honor that loyal man of mine.

I found a panel, a cotton print
With subtle red, white, and blue in it.
It had a symbolic bald eagle
Flying over mountains, so regal;
An American flag, waving high;
And three soldiers sharing the sky.

The picture was perfect, then the border;
First a marbled red was in order.
Next the blue fireworks design.
Last came the quilting when I had time.
Stitching and stitching the days away;
It was gifted on Veteran's Day.

The Old Soldier loved the gift
With his "dog tags" wrapped in it

Mary Jane Lamphier
Arlington

CANDLELIGHT VIGIL

A candle fires—and then another
For each, one person there feels searing pain.
Candles—vigil—what we cannot see
Are banged-up SUVs and teen-age bodies
Lying lifeless on the ground.

Another candle flames and still another.
Mother hearts are broken with the pain.
Silent, silent pain—and silent, too,
This room: his bike—her jeans—his cap.

Patricia Buck
Grinnell

UPON THE DEATH OF MARY OLIVER

In the first light the eagle
soared over my winter garden
her head and tail white against the cloudy sky.
She circled again and then sailed
down the river with her mate,
their courtship palpable in the January cold.

I heard you died this morning.
I found the volumes
and read your poems till I had to stop.

Walking in the snowfall
I startled and stood stock still
as the eagle perched above the river,
above a line of field stones set there to mark
the deep and shallow of a swimming hole.
The eagle watched, grew restless and flew,
disappearing down the river.
I hope she returns to fish this riffle
as the ice closes in,

so like you, Mary,
with your 'wild and precious' heart.

Nancy Parliman Schoenewe
Spencer

IMPRESSION

She pushes off with her right foot
and thrusts her left knee forward.
She is finally running again.
Mile one is difficult, but, by mile two,
it is as if she grows wings
and glides over the pavement.
Suddenly, she falls and wakes with a jolt.
She looks down and sees the phantom image
of her legs beneath the blanket.
She feels the breeze, one last time.
Just a dream.

Bailey Primus
Steamboat Rock

FOREVER NIGHT

This glare, the sun, is crouching
A child making mischief, running wild
My heart is too much like a pink sun, dragging to the very top of the sky
Then wilting blue and black on quick descent
In these labored efforts at breathing strangled in the smallest light I try
Closed eyes and drooped head
This sun feigns dead, but burning bright energy can stop for no one
The sun changes colors, shedding petals and bares the insanity within
For this day grieves with deep heavy groans
The sky heaves down and the world recoils, it is coming down low
Each creature wonders if this is the end, creation is bent as I lose my best friend
What's more it is pulsing and pangs
The world deflated, clouds gently hang
It is letting go of this sweet ball of
Love, miscarries, rolls
Heaven drips blood

Mary Schiotis
Cresco

DOCKED AT SIX MONTHS

I was largely afraid to see her
on my way to the NICU.
The car door propped me up what with
my feet hardened as cement
and legs wobbly as a spent top.
All voices were as underwater
"Red Light, Green Light, Mother May I"…stop?
I tried to drown my weighty assumptions
and float past my basic instincts,
unsee what I had seen
and baptize the picture of her in my head.
The air was stifling, suffocating, unsure footing ahead
Slipped tethering, unauthorized mooring,
would I know her in her bed?
Signing in to her unit, "understand, don't bring your
cough and cold, trim your nails and wash your hands."
All told, no universal precaution will save her if you fail.
Alas the plucky little miracle that survived the technology,
and triclosan lay in utter magnificence legs firmly planted
as tiny trees, eyes like pristine pools, unafraid to see me.

Angela J Olney
Boone

SECONDS

There is no present,
only future only past,
the seconds go by faster than
the human mind can grasp.

In the second that it takes
for the mind to comprehend,
it is in that very second that,
that second meets its end.

Make good use of all your minutes,
all your hours, all your days
but treasure all your seconds
even as they fly away.

Without those very seconds
time would come to an end
and it was with that first second that
God made time begin.

Val Weaver
Des Moines

TOMORROW'S SUN

Church spires, power lines and naked trees
snag the cloaks of fleeing spirits
rushing past on the heavy wind
shreds them into feathered tatters
that flutter to the ground like snow

This wet east wind finds a home in my chest
freezing my heart with terror
Once-glad memories now taste oddly like grief

Now the white soft whispering piles
conceal the dark treachery of ice
the hard unmelting truth
about tomorrow's sun
We know it won't be warm enough

Glen Braddy
Carroll

FROZEN SILENCE

In the stillness of an Iowa night, I wake up with an urge
to sneak outside. Nose glued to a frosty window,

I witness the white cotton candy street where
wild rabbit footprints staple the yard's pristine snow.

I run to another window, scanning the ghost makeup
under a moon-hidden sky, my body, sleepwalking,

wades into the snow – more like a foamy latte,
where tree and bush appear as jagged cake frostings.

Mind surveys the white blanket covering the cold --
then the gloomy blackness above. Frozen silence

digs into me while the stark night's color contrasts
compete for my divided attention: Where am I?

Back at my window again, still in a daze, wondering
how I wandered off into this black and white scene

of earth and sky's interconnectedness – seeming like
opposites, yet actually giving rise to one another.

Tomorrow I'll wake up to Dawn's birth from Sun's womb
and remember Nature's Yin and Yang balance.

Maryam Daftari
Fairfield

LOST IN 1960

I bought my first car spring of 1960,
a beauty she was, a two-tone green
'53 Oldsmobile, belonging to a pastor,
in pristine condition.

I kept it washed and waxed, never
a spot of dirt, never a blemish. I walked
proud amongst my peers, admired
by many for the beauty I possessed.

A downpour that day in 1960, the road
slick and wet. I went into a skid and slid
sideways off the road, throwing me out
to lie face down in the mud as it rained.

A stranger spotted the car and found me
wandering aimlessly down a gravel road.
He picked me up, injured and covered
in mud; he took me to the hospital.

I woke from a concussion a few days later,
never to remember that day. A vacant space
among the wrinkles of my brain. A day lost.

Marvin D Vallier
Council Bluffs

IRELAND, 1850'S

A long time ago
In a little Irish town
Walked an Irish lady
Leading a lad around.

"One…two…three…and four.
'Tis a shamrock I have found.
One, two, three and four,
Here, I have another
To share with you and
Make your heart merry
As we walk around together.
Come now, Freddie,
Take my hand…"

He watched her walk
And sing and play
And got a shamrock
From her each day.

This is how my grandfather,
Fredrick Carey, and my great
Grandmother, started each day.

Ronald Kahl
Burlington

MARVELOUS MADELYN

Large brown eyes with long, wispy lashes
pink cheeks and rosebud lips—
a two-year-old face framed with soft curls

That sober nature is changing;
she is beginning to understand—
her sweetness brings out the best in us

She totters toward us smiling:
her 'language' comes in shiny bursts
and seems to help her stay upright

Her words are still a mystery,
but her facial expressions reveal wisdom,
trust, strength, hope.

Hollie Roberts
Jefferson

RED RAIN BOOTS

Her rusty colored hair hung in long waves
like
a windsock being blown by a breeze.
Hazel eyes, the color of a field ready to be harvested,
sparkled
when she stared out the window.
A single dimple on the right side of her face
giving
herself away
when she was truly happy.
Pulling
on her red rain boots
she
headed out to take on the world,
one footstep
at a time.

LeAnn Hoeg
Grundy Center

FLAMING RED

Amid pulsating change
Wisps of fire besiege my heart
Innate by right
Cognizant of power
Melts our fibers

He
My refuge
My pulse
Abides within

Seduced by light
Dignifies omnipotent
Love
The purest form

Janine Ambrose
Waterloo

ANDREA BY THE NUMBERS

1 week on the job, I see
6'2" stunning blonde beauty
1,000 miles, my heart flies
½ second glances, else I'd stare
5 months on the job, we join marketing group
3 meetings and we're paired for project
6 one on one talks to discuss promotion
6 word sentences else my tongue fails me
4 month delay in project
4 months I ache
1 more meeting to continue project
1 week after the fact, I learn she's gone
10 months total, I knew her
2 months later, I learn she's still in town
1 year, 4 months later, her apartment is for rent
2 months after the fact, I learn she's
1800 miles and
2 time zones away
1,000 miles, my heart falls
1,000,000 years and more to miss her

Stephen L Brayton
Carlisle

LOIS

A woman strong and steady with a Bible in her hand
   and a prayer upon her lips
   that some might come to understand.

As she stitches with a needle on a quilt she's sewn alone,
   God has stitched her life together
   in a patchwork of His own.

The colors of her Life's Quilt show arrays of many hues
   from the Dark days and the Gray days,
   through the days of brighter Blues.

To the Reds and Orange of sunsets
   and the Greens of fields she's strolled
   while the Pastels of her lifetime are placed as they unfold.

There's the Yellow of the sunshine God has
   generously bestowed,
   and the Purple piece she treasures most
   that represents Christ's robe.

In time she'll walk the streets of Gold
   that shine with Holy Light,
   and wear as has been promised,
   a gown of spotless White.

Kathleen Russell
Ames

ELLA

She wore her hair in deep-set waves.
It was 1938; I was nine, she was eighteen.
Wearing a fancy dress and high heels,
she'd twist around to check the seams in her hose.
They had to be right in the middle of the leg;
otherwise, you would look bow-legged…even I knew that!
The entire ritual of getting ready for a date fascinated me.
She tolerated me and my admiration.
"Now don't touch my stuff," she cautioned as she went downstairs.
Of course you know, I did touch her stuff.
The appeal of it all was tantalizing for a girl of nine.

It is now 2018; she has half a room in a nursing home.
A hearing aid doesn't really help her,
so, I use a dry erase board to communicate.
It's questionable how long that will work;
macular degeneration is taking over.
When asked, "How's everything?"
always with humor, she replies,
"Well, I'm not getting any younger."
Eighty years later and I'm still admiring her!

Viola Hill
Ida Grove

GRANDPA O'MALLEY

Born on a farm at the edge of town
A healthy young lad, never a frown
But as he grew up alas, alack
He had a huge hump on his back

Raised four kids, with a devoted wife
Blessed was he, a very long life
As he grew old, wrinkled and gray
The hump on his back was there to stay

The town grieved, Grandpa O'Malley died
Lay him flat on his back the undertaker tried
Nothing worked, he said, "Help me Lord
I'll tie him down with a heavy cord"

Family and friends gave him their best
An open casket was his request
The Priest thrust his hands to the skies
Shouted, some day we all will rise

Church shook, cords broke, O'Malley rose
Organist leaped past the first three rows
People panicked, rushed out in a lurch
Grandpa O'Malley in an empty church

Merle Newman
Ankeny

GRANDPARENTS' HOME

A smell pulls at my nose and brings back a flood of memories,
that slight musty smell of my grandparents' home.
The house held so many wonderful memories,
only time pushes them out of my aging mind.
Coffee was always on the brew,
desserts often a "would you like" away.
Grandma made the best sugar cookies in the world,
and other homemade goodies I couldn't pass up.
We would lounge on the couch to watch reruns,
or sit around the table and talk about the past.
Grandpa's puzzles were his signature mark,
the care of their game farm was their devotion.
How I would love to go back and have one more day.

Anthony A Bengston
Independence

DEAR FRIENDS

As we pass our days
In self-absorption and routine
We take for granted
That your presence will always exist
Time to make memories
Complete conversations
Schedule events
To bring us together

And then, in the space
Of the beating of hummingbird wings
All is gone
Promises never kept
Will remain so
Leaving behind disbelief
And the realization of empty space
Where your breaths once flowed

Frann Ostroff
Coralville

TODAY, WE LOST A FRIEND

We received the dreaded news today;
A friend and loved one was taken away.
With feelings of hollow emptiness inside,
We need you, Precious Lord, to be our guide!

We prayed so earnestly that You would heal!
Today's dreaded news seems so unreal.
Lord, we cannot help but question, "Why?"
Experiencing such sadness, we need time to cry.

Then turning and looking to You, we realize,
Our friend and loved one is with You in Paradise.
While we will miss him, this certainly is so;
You had a far better place for him to go!

So what's left now for us to do or say?
But to follow your Word; trust and obey.
Lord, thank you once again for teaching us
The importance of where we keep our trust!

In loving memory of our friend.

Fred W De Jong
Oskaloosa

WHO I AM

Who am I?
I am an accumulation of my experiences,
The good, the bad, the ugly.
I am who I have been, who I am currently, and who I will become.
Who I have been framed who I am today.
Who I am today frames who I will be in the future.
Who I will be in the future frames how others will remember me.
Who will I choose to be?
My experiences,
The good, the bad, the ugly.
All make me who I am.

Jill Friestad-Tate
Polk City

MAY WE BECOME BLESSED

My are they blessed!
They who walk with the LORD
Walk without blame they do walk

My are they blessed!
They who speak with the LORD
Speak without shame they do speak

May we become they who are steadfast in praise
One with the LORD are they blessed

Without blame they consider
The commands --- they do keep
Without shame they do learn
The LORD's law --- they obey

May we become they who do right and no wrong
One with the LORD they are blessed

May we become they who are blessed
They who show us the way to obey
One with the LORD we become blessed

My are we blessed!
We who become they --- steadfast in praise!
One with the LORD may all become blessed!

James Roth
Eagle Grove

ON A DAY IN SPRING

I would like to die on a day in spring,
  with freshets newly gurgling in the gutters,
  tires slishing past through puddled streets,
  and skateboards scraping by.

All through this bitter winter
  you have gripped my hand,
  not ready yet to let me go.

But now together we will watch for signs:
  musky thawing earth and first-cut grass,
  sweetest honeysuckle, lilac, plum
  wafting in the blue and yellow air.

And when the oriole plumps his orange breast
  proclaiming new beginnings from the lush crabapple bough,
  then, knowing you are spent for love of me,
  I will with joy let go my final breath
  And we will rest.

Patricia Moe
Albert City

PROMISE

Grass will come again,,
vibrant, greener than pistachio and tea leaves.
Pulsing, voluptuous buds
on the survivor ash tree.

Multiple conquerors of winter's fierce death touch.
Pupil of eye widens.
Peripheral side admits
light; reflects spectacular vista.
Heart, depth remembers.
Wait.

Mary McManus
Des Moines

A SPECIAL SKILL

Punxsutawney Phil is held aloft
by the man in a funny hat.
The crowd cheers for spring
coming early while ol' Phil
blinks sleepily, bored with the noise
ready to go back to bed.
What strange rituals humans
keep to triumph over winter.
Too bad they haven't developed
any ability to hibernate 'til spring
comes in its own sweet
burst of green.

Betsy Brant
Cedar Falls

SPRING

Spring - what a wonderful time
Grass turning green
Flowers popping up
Tulips flourishing
Baby calves frolicking in the pasture
Baby goats romping in the pen
Tiny rabbits nesting in the grass
Ducklings paddling on the lazy river
Downy chicks under the warming light.
Shedding winter coats,
Donning spring jackets
Sprucing up the house.
Surprise snowstorm…
Putting on winter coats…

Janet Branson
Hartley

DAFFODILS OF APRIL

Wordsworth wrote of daffodils;
crowds of blossoms standing proud.
They didn't count on April snows
to cover all with blanket white.

What will become of anxious blooms
encased in this cold, pristine quilt now?
Will they recover from nature's blunder
to treat us to their royal show?

For many the flowers speak of survival
with life emerging from cold, cold ground.
The bulbs, when planted in the autumn,
bring pleasure, in springtime, to all around.

Take heart, then, worriers of the nations,
when cold and snow seem to know no end.
The bulbs will flower in their own time,
later on life's river, just around the bend..

Rodney Reeves
Burlington

THE FIRST

I'd know that swoop anywhere
the springtime slide
from wire or roof or barren tree
a beam of heaven touching me
descending low on grass just green.
So blessed am I amid this scene—
over now the winter wake
open now the living gate
that beckons empty souls like mine
to come at last and fully dine
to feast with eyes and grateful heart
and praise the Maker of such art
for beady eye and walnut head
for bob and hop and breast of red
for wings of gray mixed up with brown
and for that merry morning sound
but mostly for such joy unknown
when my first robin comes back home.

Carole Johnston
Sergeant Bluff

MAY'S RHYTHM

Soft blowing breezes,
Blue skies,
Puffy white clouds,
Sunny May days.

Lilacs permeating vapor,
Floating in the air,
Its fragrant perfume,
Overwhelming the senses.

Lilies of the Valley,
Tiny and white,
Wedding bells,
Waiting to ring.

Abundant grassy meadows,
Billowy from spring rains,
A field of carpet,
Cushioning bare feet.

Melodious cardinals
Frolic and chirp,
All wonderful gifts,
In the month of May.

Marie Sullivan
Cedar Rapids

SUMMER . . .

gardening, beach books, walking, biking, weeding, painting, singing, digging,
driving, dreaming, being planted in time, mourning and rejoicing, homemade pie
deck time, hummingbirds, wild turkeys on parade, dragonflies and tadpoles,
mountains, big skies, ocean waves, clouds over the valley, early morning mist,
late night fog, quiet highways, steamy afternoons, the smell of rain,
lightening in the northern sky, moonlight and starlight, ripples on the pond,
prairie grasses, endless corn fields, ghost players, night eyes,
the woods — lovely, dark, and deep.

music camp, quartets, concerts, rehearsals, performances, audience cheers,

teamwork, thunderstorms off the bay, sunsets, hawks and ospreys,
picnics with potato salad and hamburgers, friendships set to music.

"Follow me, grandma. I'm the leader. I HAVE the map!" hiking, gorilla watching,
baseball — "It's a shame, if we don't win," sunscreen and bug spray, swimming,
breakfast by the creek, pancakes with raspberry syrup, State Fair, food and
crowds,
honeybees and baby lambs, rain and more rain, sleepovers, pitching tents,
listening to night noises, answering "why" a million and one times, laughing,
whining, wishing time to slow, catching my breath, being grateful.

Kathy Meyer
Winterset

SO PROUDLY WE HAIL

In the milky dusk of the darkening sky,
constellations begin to appear
at the Annual Fourth of July Gala.

The masses below huddle on blankets,
as growing anticipation hangs heavy
in the sultry mid-summer air.

The last flicker of twilight is finally
swallowed by the black night.
Jubilant rockets take the sky by surprise!

Showers of sparkles paint the landscape
with broad stripes of patriotic colors,
while uninvited storm clouds begin arriving.

Oh say can you see such a flurry now
as deafening thunder loudly claps
and bright lightning smiles jaggedly.

Spectators race to safety,
grasping wet blankets and
small hands, hot with candy-stickiness.

All stream home, thankful to those brave
who have kept our beloved America safe and free.

Linda Dolphin
Dubuque

SUMMER

When most people look forward to summer,
Its usually warm weather, swimming in the lake,
    or barbecues with family.
Me there is only one thing on my mind.
A fresh iowa grown tomato.
I don't care if beefsteak or goliath.
Cherry or grape.
Even heirloom or lemon boy.
Just brush the dirt off and grab the salt shaker.
The first bite still warm from the sun beating on it.
The juices trickling down your chin.
Some people plan vacations,
Some look forward to relaxing,
Me, i prefer the simpler things in life.

Emily Crouse
Ottumwa

HOW TO SWAT A FLY

Have you ever tried to swat a fly?
They move fast, but I have to try!

We had so many flies on the farm
That swatting was hard on my arm.

Over the years I have tried many times,
Now I just sit and write educational rhymes.

Once I read some facts about flies.
They actually have over one hundred eyes!

That lets them see in every direction;
I have a plan to get their attention.

The swatter I lower V-E-R-Y S-L-O-W,
She watches as I get it very low.

The swatter has to be two inches above her head.
Up any higher and she will have already fled!

The grocery store belt had stopped one day.
With messy sweet stuff to eat, the fly did stay.

Picking up that long narrow divider,
Just two inches up and then I plied her!

That fly never knew what happened,
But the customers just burst out laughin'.

Alma Tallman
Atlantic

SMALLNESS

I stepped on the sidewalk
wary -- sensitive to the workers below
carrying food home to the family
as I carried mine home
to my one story flat
three rooms and a bath
theirs clutched tightly in their jaws
mine held tightly to my body
heavy with the weight of jars
only food - but theirs
building material for their nests
I tiptoed around them
my shadow at times obscuring them
the jars rattled
I watched their blackness scurrying
no, not to the grass
there, they would be invisible to me
just step slowly
gingerly
you might be next

Denise Roth
Iowa City

TADPOLE TRAVAILS

Hundreds of tadpoles swim around, going nowhere,
spooked if I get too close or cast a shadow on them.
They're small critters, half the size of a dime,
with round dark bodies and pointy tails.
These frogs-in-waiting,
congregate near the water's edge,
not knowing what lies beyond their view.
Their life's purpose is simple,
eat algae and other greenery
until they become bigger tadpoles.
An oblivious existence untainted by
the daily news, the sickness of a friend,
or the loss of a loved one.
Their lives are almost enviable,
but I know something the tadpoles don't.
Their world is actually a large puddle,
situated in a low spot on the bike path.
A precarious location, subject to the whims of rain,
curious onlookers and hungry birds.

Mark Steven Lucas
Bettendorf

DANGEROUS HOMEMAKER

Little bird, a risk-taker you must be
Little mama, just the opposite of me

You built that nest in a precarious place,
You must be counting on Heavenly grace

Little bird, three small eggs in a sturdy nest
Little mama, I know you've done your best

But surely in the future you must learn
You could all drown living in my asparagus fern!

Sandra L Green
Tipton

WOOD DUCK FAMILY

A momma wood duck uses a hollow opening
in the trunk of the ancient red oak
behind our house
for her nest each year.
When it is time to leave the nest,
the ducklings make a leap of faith
from 20 feet in the air
into our backyard.
When they are all on the ground,
I open the wooden gate
and gently herd the little family
into the pasture.
Momma hisses and flaps her wings to protect her babies
until they are clear of the fenced area.
I pause to watch another new wood duck family
waddle off into the woods.

William P Riddle
Colfax

DEEP INTO A STAR

God sure made good sense
When he graced us with their presence
They're an embodiment of all that's
Good and pure of body, heart, mind, spirit
And soul
And you don't even need to take a poll
To find out how popular and wonderful they truly are
Just look deep into a star
Of course
I'm talking about the horse
Whether the equines are domestically mild
Or wilderness wild
I will beyond eternity endorse
THE HORSE

PJ Bradway
Red Oak

THE VIEW

I'd like to show you the unending sky
   from south to north
     on old Route One.

acres of bean and corn fields
   from spring green to autumn rust
     maturing in season
simple beauty where you won't live
   muted colors, forest greens, ochre,
     a little red in the autumn

Now it's first snow, crystalline blue-white
over corn stubble and top soil
dreaming new growth.

Jacqueline Signori
Fairfield

A WINTER BLESSING

Ah, what is so sweet
As a day of rest
To a tired teacher
Who feels strangely blessed
When wind is howling
And snow is flying
And the telephone rings
As kids are lying
All snug in their beds
Dreams of Nintendo
Flashing in their heads?

Dashing to the phone
Teacher hears a voice say
"Go back to bed,
There's no school today!"

Betty Medema
Rock Rapids

CHORES

Bringing cows in for chores was a responsibility,
It was a hike and an adventure;
One December evening doing our thing,
My sister slipped and fell in the creek
On her back. She thrashed and gurgled,
Gained the bank and said don't tell daddy.
Well, she squished when she walked;
No keeping the accident quiet.
A change of clothes, back to chores.
Daddy queried why we said nothing.
We figured he'd be mad, and he was.

Carolyn Yates Reid
Letts

OUR CHRISTMAS TURKEY RAN AWAY

He jumped out of the roasting pan,
Ran down the street faster than we can.

I hope he doesn't get real cold,
He left his feathers for us to hold.

Naked as a Jay bird when he went,
On a special mission he himself sent.

We heard he was going to the department store
To replace the feathers he had worn before.

Perhaps a fuzzy wrap would keep him warm
In the snow and cold of Christmas morn.

After he gets his new found coat
And bright red scarf around his throat,

We hope he can have a good life,
And maybe find a nice turkey wife.

JoAnn Meyer
Clive

SNOW DAYS

in the midst of winter, post Polar Vortex

Cunning, its silence
snow drifting down
or blown around
over ice
frustrating beauty

Winter takes time to acclimate
us to the fallow season
Help me remember seeds underground
are awaiting spring
no less than I am

                                                 Nancy Obermueller
                                                     Cedar Rapids

SO.......WHAT'S WITH THE WEATHER?

We've had lots of storms and
 harsh weather, both far and near.
You can pray to Mother Nature.
 I don't think she'll hear.
When it's sunny, we want rain.
 When cold, we want it hot.
We can't make the weather and
 we'll take just what we've got.
All our "stuff" that is destroyed
 in floods, or wind and rain---
won't "'mount to a hill of beans"
 when Jesus comes again.
Our Creator knows just what He's doing.
 Trust Him, please.
Talk to Him about the weather,
 while down on your knees.

                                                     Dorothy E Glad
                                                           Boone

TIMELESS

The clock strikes twelve to maddening cheers
New Year bells ring out across the plains.
We who count months, days, and years
mark off what's gone and what remains.

Out in the night all seems unmoved
The landscape still and snowy dressed
The trees and clouds are unbemused
And stars shine on quite unimpressed.

William Hudson
Davenport

JANUARY'S FESTIVE FLING

My fingers and toes are totally froze.
Oh, how mightily that fierce north wind does blow,
Only adding to the pile of my wintry woes!
Surrounded by scenes of glittering snow,
Surrendering to artfully dancing over the glistening ice.....
Amazing! This surely must be Iowa's version of January nice

Rose E Morgart Elsbecker
Marshalltown

JANUARY, DINNER HOUR

After the snow fell deep
blew into draws
mounded over stumps
glinted by sunny day
and settled under slate sky
late in the afternoon
the deer would arrive.

Three does stepped gingerly
across the crusted woodland floor.
A young buck—four points--
kicked up a cloud of snow
chasing last spring's twins
down the ridge.

They gathered, cautiously,
where seeds and corn speckled the snow
and, letting hunger rule nerves,
ate their fill at the cold-laid table.

Jean Thomson
Mount Pleasant

WINTER'S REPRIEVE

Cold, record, cold.
Polar vortex parked in my drive.

Floral patterns on frosted window panes.
Perfect snow dogs indicative of the day's frigidity.
Breath freezes your nose hairs, icicles form in your beard.
Heavy boots hiding warm toes in thermal socks.

Embers glowing in the wood stove,
Steaming coffee mug warms chilled fingers.
Pets look out the window longingly,
Returning to their warm nest for another nap.

Optimism springs abundant. The Postman came.
Leaving dreamy seed catalogs in the box.
Green beans, sweet corn, plump tomatoes.
Making your mouth water with desire.

The grip of Winter's icy hand,
Suspended for a moment.

Mark Armstrong
Waukon

OUTSIDE

It is so very, very cold outside.
My fingers and my toes outside
Are as cold as is my nose outside.
Why am I still here outside?

The wind is blowing hard outside,
"Round and 'round my yard outside.
The sidewalks and the drive outside
Are high and high with snow outside.

I shovel, shovel, push outside,
Here and there and yon outside,
And then around the bend outside.
No sight I see in end outside.

I heave and heave the snow outside,
Piled up to the sky outside,
This is so in vain outside.
I must be insane outside!

On second thought, to be outside,
I'd rather take my leave outside
To sit inside and see outside
This wondrous wintry world…outside!

Patti Collins
Montezuma

THE DEMISE OF MY MAILBOX

The door on the front
hung down from its hinges
like the tongue of an old hound dog.

The other end blew
off its weld and buried
itself in the snow bareback.

Both sides spraddled out
like a bronc-rider's legs
held hard and fast at the top.

The short oak plank
that served as the bottom
was splintered, split and black.

That tough old box
of galvanized steel
fell to a prankster's plan.

One thunderous blast
took out the survivor
of many a snow-plow attack.

Sally Young
Little Rock

LAST RIGHTS

Mike can't file
any more complaints,
since he's dead,
and since he's dead,
we can't say anything
but good about him.
His carping, his whining,
his threatening, too,
all went into
the crematorium with him,
along with his smirks
and his zealotry.
If death seems the only way
to redeem reputations,
we may give thought and ask
if we're going the wrong way
on a one-way street.

Nancy Riggan
Orange City

FIRST PLACE, HUMOROUS VERSE:

POET'S DELIGHT

In the middle of the night
I wake—I write.
I sound so very erudite
Until the break of morning light.

Jo Ann Benda
Iowa City

SECOND PLACE, HUMOROUS VERSE:

FIT BIT

Don't get me a Fit Bit for Christmas.
Counting my steps – indeed!
For me it would be quite useless.
Aching joints – only measure I need.

So please don't give me that Fit Bit.
A trip to the beach will suffice
I don't give a whit about being fit.
Just get me away from this ice!

Sandra Conner Ladegaard
Arnolds Park

THIRD PLACE, HUMOROUS VERSE:

THE TALE OF THE TRAVELING TABLOID

After the newspaper was thoroughly read,
It was time to go ahead and have it shred.
Soon after, to the recycling center it sped.
Then, off to a sty to become a soft bed.

Its job now finished, it's certainly dead.
The black print turned to manure in the shed.
But, wait, onto a wheat field it's been spread.
Who knew a newspaper could turn into bread?

Mary Jedlicka Humston
Iowa City

FIRST HONORABLE MENTION, HUMOROUS VERSE:

"I SAID, A-CHOO! NOT, I DO!"

Here I lie dead,
fertilizing my grass bed.
While I slowly decompose,
'Twas her cooking, I suppose.

Here I repose,
worms boring holes in my nose.
Reads the stone crushing my head:
WHY DID I WED?

Mary Bolin
Ankeny

SECOND HONORABLE MENTION, HUMOROUS VERSE:

EAGER TO SAVE

I grab my purse and head to the market.
Pull into the lot in my car and park it.

Through the automatic door I dart
straight to the stall for a cart.

Up and down each aisle I peruse.
Mentally matching coupons to items I use.

At checkout I discover with horror
I left my coupons at home in a drawer.

Helen J Thoen
Manly

THIRD HONORABLE MENTION, HUMOROUS VERSE:

THE RUSH

From the moment your foot hits the floor
Your ear hears the slam of car door
The bladder shouts "hurry"
Down the hall you must scurry
Or you'll be changing your duds once more.

Marylyn L Gillespie
Lake City

SLICK SALESMAN

There was a slick salesman in disguise
Who always liked a new surprise
One day into cement he fell
And became known as the "Hard Sell."

Norman Wolfe
Stuart

SONG OF THE LAZY HOMEMAKER

The day is here, the day is new
Now tell me please, what shall I do?

The tasks are clear that should be done.
All I need do is just pick one.

The list is long and growing still.
The list is stronger than my will,

And so I think I'll lie abed
Until I get the paper read.

Joan Daily Rammelsberg
Marion

PANTS

What ever happened to pants that come up to your waist?
Everywhere I look today I think it's a disgrace.
When people are always hitching, trying to pull them into place?
There are things we shouldn't see that are parts of the human race;
But who am I to rebel since I certainly do not choose to wear
Anything so uncomfortable? I wouldn't think of buying only a hip high pair
Of pants or jeans that I can't keep up without wearing long suspenders.
To this type of "designer" clothes I simply won't surrender!

Melba Muhlenbruch
Hampton

HARD BARGAIN

I bought a cheap, used car
and much to my chagrin,
I found how difficult
to drive a hard bargain!

Ellen Danner
Woodburn

DEATH BY IAMBIC PENTAMETER

Some
poets
of great skill
say that to write
an iambic line
is as natural to
our inner self as breathing:
In. Out. In… But, for me, writing
iambic verse is much like choking
to death, just one syllable at a time.

Frank Kutchen
Des Moines

A FAIRY TALE?

"Cinderella, dressed in yellow," was a jump rope rhyme.
What color pretty Ella wore is lost in long gone time.

Weeping sadly Ella sat the night of Charming's Ball.
When suddenly a fairy came to dress her, hair and all.

A golden coach whisked her away. She was a lovely sight
With gown more regal than the rest. The other girls took flight.

The gossip bloomed, "Who was that girl?" Yet Ella smiled quite smugly.
She had her Ball and danced with all. The Prince was very ugly.

Edy Fudge
Clive

FIRST PLACE, SONNETS:

SONNET TO MYSELF

At fifty-nine I celebrate myself
Like Whitman, but with softened leaves of grass
Another year I place upon the shelf
And reckon with the woman in the glass.

She's loosened now, with silky feathered skin
She's rounder with her words; her diatribes
Once sharp and clawed, now blunted from within
As to the mild thought she now ascribes.

October curve around the lap of life
Has rounded edges, plumped accepting ways.
The scalpel is replaced with putty knife.
The truth, now slant, is told in sunset rays.

A softer, rounded life at fifty-nine
I celebrate the gentle arc of time.

Allison Berryhill
Atlantic

SECOND PLACE, SONNETS:

THE QUILTER

Near one small unincorporated town
she learned to quilt in early days of youth.
Without seeking status or renown
her essence spoke of modesty and truth.
She was never anything but kind
and as her children grew in stature
they matured with thoughtful open minds
true reflections of their mother's nature.
The hours spent toiling at her quilting frame
to her, were neither wearisome nor dull.
With perfect stitches she fulfilled her aim
creating quilts both warm and colorful.
    Serenity and faith refined her life,
    A dedicated quilter, mother, wife.

Betty Taylor
Hartley

THIRD PLACE, SONNETS:

POND (No. 4)

It's almost spring and sixty-two degrees!
My day of birth, I'm sixty-two today!
TyOhni charges toward our pond to seize
the day. He scares a pair of geese away.
They circle overhead and leave. Atop
the bank is elegance, a heron bends
with graceful, lengthy neck and legs, it stops,
until our dog pursues the bird which sends -

Ascending skyward toward the brilliant blue,
Enormous wing span, effortless in flight;
Magnificence above me, who are you?
A prehistoric presence or the might
of great Houdini? Absolutely this:
You are the birthday bird who brings me bliss!

Linda Wolfe
Greenfield

FIRST HONORABLE MENTION, SONNETS:

TRICKLING STREAM

It travels swiftly over bumpy rocks,
In twists and turns and waves along the trail.
It calls me to take off my shoes and socks,
To leave the bridge with feet all bare and pale.

The glistening water wakes my sense of peace
As sticks and leaves float by and draw me in.
The trials of the day I now release,
And touch the chilly sweetness on my skin.

And then, I feel the gurgle on my toes—
The sparkling splash that swirls with every stride—
Crisp, creeky air, it fills my lungs and nose,
And in these moments, worries fall aside.

Its presence and its power is like a dream.
I never want to leave my trickling stream.

Laura Sohl-cryer
Cedar Falls

SECOND HONORABLE MENTION, SONNETS:

THE BACK SIDE

Store facades gleam grandly from the street
Fashioned from the finest steel and stone.
The coiffed front lawns and houses prim and neat
Display the very best the dwellers own.
The finest decor on the Yuletide tree
Reserved as striking show for public view
Less stunning deemed the lesser in degree,
The cracked and worn deferring to the new.
The back side of the storefront features flaws
Where litter lives and where unwanted sleep,
Where unkempt back yards fail to earn applause,
Disfigured firs not memories to keep.
Why in the vain appearance we preserve
Do the less than perfect less deserve?

Lori Shannon
Manning

THIRD HONORABLE MENTION, SONNETS:

AUTUMN IN IOWA

When the woodbine twining fence and tree turns red,
Clacking cornstalks mark the rhythm of our walk.
When puddles reflect the blue sky overhead,
And football is the heart of local talk,
Leaves like golden coins are swept along.
They end a trailing shawl on country roads.
The hum of distant combines is a song
That celebrates the reaping of the sowed.
Mist hovers on the river down below,
Ethereal to those of us above.
Rain intensifies the autumn calico
Becoming the rich colors that we love.
We hold on to autumn's beauty as we know
We'll face the test of winter's ice and snow.

Christine Brink
Dow City

ON PATIENCE

King George decreed that to the course we stay
For all, says he, will come to those who wait.
While villain Time consumes our precious day
With idle promise and a slothful gait.

Our piteous raging does not make peace come
Despite our everlasting futile hammering.
Old Time just smiles and sits upon his thumbs
And listens to the din of useless yammering.

This endless waiting does not character build
When calm and carefree days are our desire
The end of conflict keeps our thoughts fulfilled,
To sweet conclusion's peace do we aspire.

No, patience's not a truly wondrous thing
For its abuse anesthetized the king.

Diane Benzing
Neola

16 YEARS

I complain to my mother about you
How you don't bother to shut dresser drawers
Or when I'm overwhelmed, you don't have a clue
My feelings you so often ignore.

The counter overflows with dirty dishes
You said you would do to help me out.
You dump junk in everyone of my niches
And when I won't clean up after, you pout.

Amateur plumber and handyman
"Fixing" all parts of the house, again,
Then resting on a couch under a fan
I collapse at your side in your den.

Wrapped in your arms, my complaints cease
And my love for you begins to increase.

Emily DeYoung
Nevada

OH, APRIL—2018

Oh, April where are you? By chance,
Caged 'neath nature's plague, I fear.
For don't you know, for you, I've saved this dance?
But, out of step, lest you've forgotten I am here.

The snowy rain is falling 'round about,
Though yesterday seemed promise of bright shine,
And so you puzzle me and cause me doubt.
Are you losing heart and breaking mine?

Years past we ran together in the fields,
Hop-scotched, jumped rope and roller-skated.
But, looking out my window only yields,
Fond memories, now your presence so belated.

Bright sunshine, April dear, is waiting now,
If you don't know how to dance, I'll show you how.

Eleanor Stenzel
Burt

THE LONG JOURNEY HOME

It has been a long journey since December third,
they passed the death sentence, we both heard every word.
I fought it in disbelief knowing they were wrong.
You'd be your old self before too long.
The days passed with your slow decline.
I realize now, everything isn't fine.
The sadness of your leaving is written on your face.
It won't be long now 'til you're in a better place.
I tell you when the time comes heaven will be your prize.
You look at me with doubt and worry in your eyes.
Jesus loved the blind, the lame, they were the chosen ones.
I see you with two good arms and legs when your journey's done.
Mom and Dad will be waiting to meet you face to face.
It won't be long until bagpipes play, "Amazing Grace."

Lee L Gordon
Marquette

AT MOTHER'S BEDSIDE

We grew as one, in solidarity
and poverty, though not of love deprived.
In mutuality we lived and thrived
in our cocoon. While dreams in rarity

were shared, not understood with clarity,
we twined as fibers in a rope, survived.
Our countless games and pranks revived
us from dull chores in endless quantity.

When came the day our cocoon burst apart,
we scattered. One took flight, then fluttered down;
a sister loitered longer in the nest.

Three soared, then leveled, kept a gentle heart.
Tonight the five, regrouped, are gathered round:
Farewell to her who'd held each to her breast.

Lucille Morgan Wilson
Des Moines

SPELLBOUND

CROSSWORDERS align words using their wits.
Down and across numbered boxes share clues,
Found words spur hope, so do hint-helping quips.
Last word spells success, each puzzler their due.

SCRABBLERS like mingling letters for scores,
Luck of the draw sends words every which way.
Players scheme spaces where values are more,
Suspense till the end, *"Turnabout is fair play."*

JUMBLERS arrange letters into a queue.
Sounds like? Prefix or suffix? Spelling err?
Befuddled. Dismayed. *Argh!* Alphabet stew.
VOILA! Word puzzled out, letters all square.

POETS ponder words to parse the right kind,
Puzzling the presumed in new frame of mind.

Warren Robert Reinecke
Grinnell

A SONNET FOR MY CHILDREN

A mother shares her self, her love.
This journey starts when first they meet.
Connecting earth with stars above
A child is born: tiny hands, tiny feet.

A mother knows her heart, her soul,
Meant for more than her life alone,
Grows ev'ry day into her role
To give her child a loving home.

Strongest bond: a mother, a child,
Separate lives, yet close at heart--
Lasting memories some wild, some mild
Paths lead forward when miles apart.

Love ever lasting day thru night
A mother, a child: Love's delight.

Donna Behlke
Iowa City

FIRST PLACE, HAIKU:

chickens scratch red dirt
white sheets snap in a scold-wind
coyote waiting

Dennis Maulsby
Ames

SECOND PLACE, HAIKU:

NEWBORN

The mother's tongue and
The west wind balanced the calf
On its wobbly legs.

Richard R Ramsey
Des Moines

THIRD PLACE, HAIKU:

Chinese papyrus
in a tan pottery vase
far from green marshes

Joanne Dyhrkopp Schar
Spencer

FIRST HONORABLE MENTION, HAIKU:

Sentry stag shredded
Sapling struggling to survive
Shrouded fawn scion

Tracy Edens
Iowa City

SECOND HONORABLE MENTION, HAIKU:

QUIET WORLD

Free breeze blankets me
Trees stay my sturdy coarse friends
Birds glide as leaves fall

Elizabeth Spratt
Oelwein

THIRD HONORABLE MENTION, HAIKU:

A white butterfly
Flutters on the salty breeze:
April by the sea.

Shirley Hilton
Cedar Rapids

little umbrella
opening in the sunshine —
the canopy fills

Patricia E Noeth
Iowa City

vacant baseball park
a homeless dog in outfield
still chasing mayflies

Shelly Reed Thieman
West Des Moines

Shiny scarlet orbs
cling to gnarled mountain ash limbs,
beckon doe-eyed deer.

Janet A Wiener
Hinton

Cold night, waning moon
Prayer rides on Milky Way
Shooting star burns, dies

Deborah Lewis
Ames

deceptive sunshine
winds foreshadow winter's wrath
thieves of autumn mirth

Julie Allyn Johnson
Norwalk

pale mist floods river
storm-broken limbs ride ripples
clouds blur reflection

Virginia Mortenson
Des Moines

Dawn's wide wheel of fire—
four suns realize the rim—
brightness ice-broken.

Jean M Evans
Grundy Center

the pain of grieving...
the stray cat's bowl filling up
with cold rain water

Josie Hibbing
Hartley

field mouse forages
in thatch beneath bare oak branch
patient white owl blinks

Jed Magee
Charles City

Kleptomaniac
They find always in the frost
Apples gone, jaws bare

Gabriella Piconi
Boone

a hard south wind blows
branches of sycamore dance—
the sound of woodwind

Bill Simmons
Carroll

      in the cedar tree
gossipy sparrows exchange
   rumors about spring

Milli Gilbaugh
Iowa City

out scooping the loop
testing the limit of wings
those teenage robins

Del Todey Turner
Waterloo

Long-stemmed sandhill cranes
Aggressively cry, attack,
Modern day dinosaurs

Pauline Borton
State Center

Tulip's shoulder
dripping slush
warm dirt

Tyler Hahn
Cherokee

Orange lantern moon
Soft glow sways on river waves
Lovers gaze in awe

Virginia Westbrook
Des Moines

she thought she could not
then she found her own power
now she can't be stopped

Laura Willging
Dubuque

barren tree branches
rattle and moan as wind howls
stars remain silent

Pat Bieber
Muscatine

annual delight
silks clinging, butter dripping
Iowa sweet corn

Kerrin Roelfsema Jass
Iowa Falls

newborn baby cries
wakes me in the still of night
we'll rock until dawn

Bryan Tabbert
St Ansgar

green tractor on rural road
stirs up memories
of Iowa cornfields

Roberta Beach Jacobson
Indianola

Bite juicy burger
Hold the mustard and pickle
Red splat on white shirt

Rita Lewin
Manchester

FIRST PLACE, NATIONAL/WORLD EVENTS:

A GATHERING

Voices pass over
Olive carts and dates,
Merchants bantering.

Yet the chatter
Quiets with each
Nudge, fingers pointing,
Faces now turning
To the small crowd
Yonder.

A puddle of people
Collect along the
Stone-paved street,
Swelling around
One man.

Under the shade
They listen,
A loose seed
Of mustard passed
Person to person

Jeffrey Meyer
Mount Pleasant

SECOND PLACE, NATIONAL/WORLD EVENTS:

A DAY OF MADNESS

I began to weep seeing horrors
outside the Urakami Cathedral
amid skeletons of the horrific explosion,
that scarred innocent faces,
burnt patterns on human flesh,
and melted eyes of the pure
on that August day in 1945.

The day the bells did not ring
for those disfigured by flames,
charred by unseen radiation,
or left wandering among the dead.
My tears became fears
outside Nagasaki Peace Park in 1956
seeing the insanity of igniting the air.

Joe Millard
West Des Moines

THIRD PLACE, NATIONAL/WORLD EVENTS:

WAR ENDS... 1945

A giant sleeps a restless sleep
Upon the troubled ground
His rumbling breath so loud and deep
Makes an ominous sound
A great event proclaimed his birth
Mingled with blood and gore
The atom bomb that rules the earth
Has now begun to snore

Jan Blankenburg
Donnellson

FIRST HONORABLE MENTION, NATIONAL/WORLD EVENTS:

THE LOST AND FOUND

The world stirs with news of twelve boys
and their soccer coach trapped in the caves of Thailand
with the early Monsoon. Day after day after day nothing,
yet they could be alive.

On the tenth day, one boy's birthday, divers probe,
emerge with lights shifting like a mirage on bare legs
and electric smiles from boys perched on rocks
much too close to Heaven.

Fed, tended by a doctor, scuba diving lessons,
letters to parents, leader credited with coaching calm
apologizes, starting with the one who lives the farthest,
four plus four plus five boys make it out alive.

Mourn diver lost. The world with a tsunamic sized sigh
breathes thanks to men called seals in a land called Thai.

Phyllis IT Harris
Ames

SECOND HONORABLE MENTION, NATIONAL/WORLD EVENTS:

WORLD WAR II

April 6, 1944
"Missing in action"
the telegram said.

Maundy Thursday
I walked to church
in the rain.

The unknown, now my
constant companion,
was brutal company

until midnight
January 30, 1946,
when a soldier

stepped from the
long, dark train
and into my arms.

Ramona Morse
Osage

THIRD HONORABLE MENTION, NATIONAL/WORLD EVENTS:

YOUNG JOB WELLING'S GRAVE
(FIRST COMPANY, HANDCARTS TO ZION, 1856)

Living without walls an arm's length apart
Hearing every breath every sigh or cry
They must have known when all of it stopped
When the spirit left and stillness set in
News was exchanged at crossings and rest stops
The whole camp would know before they arrived
In all the ways a hand can be extended
Those "saints" extended theirs to each other
Each one had pushed alone against the trail
Then came together 'round their evening meal
Which, repeated, became a sacrament
And then – this most sacred – love's last detail
Fell to the many, in community
And turned their labors into testaments
And loosed a faith to stiffen every will

Gene M Rohr
Grinnell

SUPER BLOOD MOON

The sun, the moon,
and the earth align.

Glowing like a pumpkin in the night sky.

Suspended in the darkness,
lighting a crimson path.

Such a rare and beautiful sight,
when the moon passes through
the earth's shadow.

Robin Ostedgaard
Iowa City

SHUTDOWN: DEC. 22, 2018 - JAN. 25, 2019

This government shutdown,
It affected way too many of us.
Workers, yes, but those on SNAP,
Meals for March they can't trust.

They're told to save their food stamps,
Try to make them last.
What if you're barely eating,
And they're still disappearing too fast?

Can we please end this madness?
Some of us can barely eat,
Hoping this shutdown won't restart,
This isn't a hopeful feat.

Brianna Smith
Council Bluffs

GRETCHEN FOSKET MEMORIAL AWARD:

POOR LITTLE KITTY

Little kitty up a tree
meowing loud and helplessly.
"Hang on kitty! Don't you cry!
I'll get you. At least I'll try!"

Broken branches snag my clothes,
jagged tree limbs scratch my nose.
Leaves get tangled in my hair.
"Here I come. I'm almost there!"

The kitty jumped right over me.
I watched him run straight down the tree.
He didn't need my help at all.
Oh no! I hope I don't fall!

I wish I never had looked down.
Am I that far off the ground?
I'm scared to move. What should I do?
I know. "MEOW!" I'll try it, too.

Joyce Allen
Ankeny

FIRST PLACE, POEMS FOR CHILDREN:

SIDEWALK ART

Savannah Sue drew a giant gnu
On Grandma's garden walk.
We dubbed him Stu and colored him blue
With enormous and bright-colored chalk.

Later that day, the sky turned to gray
And rain came down willy-nilly.
It trashed our view of Savannah Sue's gnu.
Stu began to look awfully silly.

We whispered adieu to the sidewalk tattoo,
As colors washed onto the lawn.
The swirly bright roux rejoined, "Toodle-oo!"
'Twas a portrait most lovingly drawn.

Alanna Clutter
Des Moines

SECOND PLACE, POEMS FOR CHILDREN:

BILLY THE BAT

When the night grows dark
And the skeeters come out
Billy the Bat
Goes on his route

He can't see a thing
But he sends out a sound
And flits through the air
For food to be found

He works all night long
Cause skeeters ain't much
When you have to have
Skeeters for breakfast and lunch.

He scares all the girlies
With long tresses they bare
They tremble in fright
He'll land in their hair

As the moon goes to sleep
and the sun starts to rise
Billy hangs up
And closes his eyes.

Dale Netherton
Farmington

IT'S ME

You say I look different
There has been a change
I agree too
Something is strange

When I smile real big
You can't help but see
Even though something's missing
I'm still TOOTHLESS me

Vicky Dovenspike
Salem

THIRD PLACE, POEMS FOR CHILDREN:

PLAN B

If you're feeling sad and funky
just imagine you're a monkey.

Be a funny funky monkey.

If this old world is too absurd
pretend you're a bird.

That's the word — be a bird.

If it seems you just can't win
imagine you're a happy penguin.

Grin like a penguin.

If the world seems gray and flat
a cat would not notice that.

Tell your troubles to scat like a cat.

If you are down and need a laugh
just imagine you're a giraffe.

Laugh like a giraffe.

Kathleen Hart
Fort Madison

JAKE AND THE SQUIRRELS

"Bark, bark," said Jake the Dog.
"You squirrels go away from me."
"Chee, Chee," said the squirrels,
"You're tied around our tree.
We built our home from leaves and sticks.
There on the ground are the nuts we eat.
You're standing on our food."
"Go away," said Jake, "I don't like squirrels,
go live in another tree."
The winter wind blew, the squirrels' home fell.
"We're cold," said the squirrels,
"let us come down,
We'll share those nuts with you."
Jake was hungry, the squirrels were cold.
Finally Jake's heart turned to gold.
"I'll eat those nuts and keep you warm.
Come snuggle up with me."

Carolyn Rohrbaugh
Sutherland

FIRST HONORABLE MENTION, POEMS FOR CHILDREN:

SCALES OF SHINY BLUE

Once there was a child
one very much like you
who believed himself to be a dragon
with scales of shiny blue

He stomped around the kitchen
he terrified the cat
he drank right from the fishbowl
he dug up all the plants

He tangled up his mother's yarn
in order to make a nest
he took a dirt bath in the yard
while in his Sunday best

He climbed atop a fencepost
and hissed at all who passed
then rode his bike downhill so fast
he very nearly crashed

His mother had finally had enough
and said, "What should I do?"
He told her, "Don't worry now,
tomorrow I'll be something new!"

Laura A Thompson
Postville

SECOND HONORABLE MENTION, POEMS FOR CHILDREN:

TRUE STORY

The slobbery mess that I hand to you here
is all that is left of my homework, I fear.

The dog ate my homework, I tell you - it's true!
He thought it was dog food. Hey, that's what they do.

He saw it and gnawed it and ran up the stairs
because homework is tasty and puppies don't care.

The next time that hound will be sent out to play
While the cat helps me study - or else sleeps all day.

Lindsey Smith
West Des Moines

THIRD HONORABLE MENTION, POEMS FOR CHILDREN:

MY WINTER VISITOR

I had a little visitor
on an icy winter day
He prowled around my patio
"a snack?" he seemed to say

His shape was roly-poly
and his nose was very pointy
His eyes were small and glinty
and his tail was very skinny
His claws were very sharp and flinty
his coat was grey and white – not pretty
His size was like a little dog
or maybe a fat cat – not hog!
All in all, an ugly sight!
in fact, he gave me quite a fright!
I watched him from my safe, warm room
(the ice, to him, was not a boon)
Until, at last, he slunk away,
My winter visitor of the day!

(did you guess what he was?
a 'possom!)

Cleo McKim
Mount Pleasant

THE SOAP SONG

When in water deep I sit
To rub off dirt and grime a bit,
Why does the soap float to my feet
When the other end its needs must meet?

And when I try to grab it tight,
That slippery soap dives out of sight
To depths unknown to my sponge and me!
How many places can that soap be?

It couldn't have slithered down the drain.
It must be where I can see it plain.
I don't care, it can have its fun.
My toes look wrinkly, that means I'm done!

Karen Schmitt
Solon

GOOD KING TOMMY TODDLER

Cherry Cheerios are so cherry don't you see
That the Dreaded Shredded Wheat "Quakered" in jealously.
Why should his life be round and cheery
While Shredded Wheat is square and dreary?
I'll make him see life's not been fair!
Why should he live without a care?
I'll snap his crackle
 And crackle his pop.
Breakfast of champions he is not!
But, as a new day dawned, he fell into some milk
And there was Cherry Cheerios afloat upon the silk.
Enter Tommy Toddler
King on his high chair
Demanding cereal with his spoon
poised high in the air.
Ground and round or shredded square
Tommy Toddler didn't care
He ate 'em both!

Kay Thomann
Riverside

ROOM TO SPARE!

It's time for first grade volleyball;
I'm learning how to hit.
The net we use seems extra tall;
Improving bit by bit.

I hit the ball with quite a smack;
It crashed into the net.
The goal, I know, is over the top;
I haven't got it yet.

The ball just JUMPED right off my hand
And whizzed up through the air.
It flew so high, way over the top;
With plenty of room to spare!

H Randall Hengst, II
Bettendorf

TINY WINGS

Up, up and away,
Little Hummers dip and dive,
Protect precious nectar,
Drive others away,
Tiny wings hover and hum,
Summer symphony begins.

Nancy Hanaman
Rippey

MULBERRY BLISS

Mulberries on my fingers.
Squished between my toes.
Jump up grab a branch,
be careful now, higher up I go.
Flick the little inchworm
off of my shoulder, then my arm.
Now back to the mulberries.
Mom will make us jam.
Oblong sweet and juicy.
Suck them off the stem.
Another one for the bucket.
Oh my, I've eaten ten.
Deep purple on my fingers.
Purple smile past my nose.
Gosh my feet are purple,
Even both elbows.
Love that little berry.
Tasty purple gem.

Lynn Robbins
Norwalk

OCTOBER-FEST

Jack-o-lantern toothy grins,
smiles are bright from lights within,
witches cackle in the night,
black cats howl and bats in flight.

It's thrills and chills come Halloween
with spooks and goblins roaming free,
and witches preparing their favorite brew,
black cat tails and bat wing stew.

Ghosts and ghouls return again
so put on a costume and join right in.
There's fun and games and treats galore,
and spooky stories to tell once more.

Anna Barnes
Sioux City

LITTLE FREE LIBRARY

Balance on tiptoe.
Scan through the pane
a hodgepodge collection
of tales and adventures
you can recite by heart.
Open the door and sail
once again with Max
to that untamed shore.

Annette Matjucha Hovland
Muscatine

RICHARD THE GALLANT

Richard the gallant gallops
    And prances
He charges and leaps
    In wild-horse dances.

His black mane and tail
    Flow like ocean waves.
His deep brown eyes
    Pull you into his gaze.

He races the wind
    On the plains out west.
He defies great storms,
    Rearing in protest.

Plainsmen and predators
    Don't cross his path.
Flying hooves and sharp teeth
    Display his wrath.

From atop a high hill,
    He guards his band.
Mares and foals graze
    In peace over the land.

Linda Shivvers
Des Moines

THE SNEEZE

"Achoo!" sneezes Kyle,
        my four year old,

I say, "Cover your nose,
        don't spread your cold."

Kyle replies, "I don't know whether
        I'll sneeze or ho-hum,

to get my hankie out
        would make me feel dumb."

Janet Gilchrist
Douds

SCHOOL LUNCH

Our lunch lady, Vic Vicki McNeal,
cooked us a wacky, weird school meal.
She licked the spoon; it made her choke.
Her hair stood up; her nostrils smoked.
Her toes curled up; her breath wreaked fire.
Her false teeth fell into the fryer.
Cook Deb raced in to help McNeal.
She did five flips and one cartwheel.
"No worries; I'm here," cook Deb did say.
"I'll serve the lunch and save the day!"
She stirred the pot; it made her scream.
Her eyebrows melted from the steam.
It was the strangest thing we'd ever seen.
So who will eat this crazy cuisine?
Not me! Not me! Not me!

Kim Dovel
Hamburg

IF I WERE A COOKIE...

I might be made of coconut
dipped in chocolate, like those
sold by Girl Scouts, or a plain little
cookie shaped like their emblem.

I might be a Mexican wedding cake
buttery and sweet with chopped
pecans, shaped in a ball,
rolled in powdered sugar.

Or, I might be a sandwich
of thin, pressed chocolate
wafers with a sweet, soft,
creamy vanilla filling.

On further thought, I might be
a crisp, thin cookie—sprinkled
with red or green sugar crystals
in celebration of Christmas.

Of course, if I were a plate,
I'd want to offer a selection
of all these cookies, as well as
the traditional chocolate chip.

Janis Stone
Ames

THE RAIN COMES DANCING

The rain crept not, but strode right in,
Counting insects to be shushing.
With taps it makes its entrance grand,
Gently stymies with each blessing.

Wobbling a waltz with the thunder,
Smoke trees shudder without a sound.
Their leaves like crimson cymbals crash
As they stroll the horizon round.

John Snethen
Williamsburg

THREE WISHES

I spied a green bottle in waves by the shore
A blue genie appeared like of Aladdin's lore
A red turban with emeralds and diamonds galore
An orange vest with rubies and pearls he wore
Then he granted three wishes as in legends of yore
I thought about candy, I'd own my own store
Maybe dollies, bikes and kites that would soar
I thought about maids to do all my chores
And puppies, ponies or lions that roar
I thought about money, so I'd never be poor
Then I thought of things I took for granted before
All of my blessings and things I adore
My family, friends, pets and much more
My home, church, school and the stores
I thought about freedoms America affords
So I tossed that green bottle into the sea's roar
And prayed that it land on some distant shore
Where people are suffering the ravages of war
That some child will be granted what she's wishing for

Valrie Schuster
Shell Rock

FIRST PLACE, COLLEGE:

THE NEW KID ON THE BLOCK

so they asked me to write a poem to you
I'm not really sure what to say, in such an event
what to unleash to another, the world so new
I'm sorry they picked me, I'm sorry I was sent

you've chosen an odd time to become
the nation unraveling, the president raging
the globe melting, everyone somehow numb
to a revolution my generation is changing

but honestly, welcome I suppose, I guess
to this wonderful planet, to this somber day
I hope you'll grow up, and make use of our mess
we tried to fix a system broke, to make our say

by the time you've reached an angsty teen
the world will have changed a whole heap
but for now I leave you, a small warm bean
I pray your sanity, and your innocence, you keep

Albie Nicol
Cedar Falls, IA
University of Northern Iowa, Cedar Falls

SECOND PLACE, COLLEGE:

THE RIVER STYX

The warehouse lights reflect upon the sur-
face of the river, wav'ring spectres of
blue and yellow incandescence. They shake
and waver with the waters, glinting as
if in a trance. They dance and lurch but can-
not flee, just stretch their flighty fingers to
the cold, uncaring shore. And when they think
they've almost touched the stone of land, it's lurched
back to the water's grasp to stay entrapped
in somber mourning, ever waltzing to
a tune that's doomed to never reach the end.

Anneke Wind
Johnstown, CO
Dordt College, Sioux City

THIRD PLACE, COLLEGE:

FROM THE CHURCH PEW

I didn't hold her hand
because I knew we weren't allowed.

I didn't play footsie with her
because it would have felt dirty in such a sterile place.

I didn't look over at her
when the pastor addressed our secret sin.

I didn't know what to do
when she wiped a tear away.

I didn't put a comforting hand on her thigh
like I wanted to.

She didn't meet my eyes
when I looked over.

I stayed still
when she left to make sure no one saw her cry

and I opened my hymnal like the pastor commanded
voiceless.

Anneliese Donstad
Tomball, TX
Dordt College, Sioux City

SEETHING

Door slams—hard. The bedroom window rattles.
Seconds later—pounding. The door rattles.
Then—low, un-yielding words that I choose to ignore,
—words heard so many times before.

My head lands on the pillow— two wet spots already forming on the fabric,
mixing with black mascara. Tears not from sadness—never sadness—
but from self-righteous anger and relentless unfathomable frustration.
Slow breaths, slow breaths—before you say something you'll regret.

Danielle Schultz
Fountain, MN
Dordt College, Sioux City

FIRST HONORABLE MENTION, COLLEGE:

JUMBLED

The wall that holds
her tired arms.
The dainty elbows that
take on the weight of the day.
The casual posture in her frame,
on the phone.
The coffee in her mug about to spill over.
A hat to cover the stray hairs
that frame her pale white face.
Her shoulders droop.
Her face holds a look of concern.
The books that fill this room
would not hold the
stories that her
draping form tells.

Katie Bousema
Escondido, CA
Dordt College, Sioux City

SECOND HONORABLE MENTION, COLLEGE:

IN
THE LIBRARY

Knights
 dance against parchment landscapes.
Presidents
 thunder, con-men sing.
The
 princess saves herself.

Hannah Adams
Sheboygan, WI
Dordt College, Sioux City

His piercing blue gaze
Slowly drifted far away
Never seen again

Ashley Kochuyt
Atkins, IA
Clarke University, Dubuque

THIRD HONORABLE MENTION, COLLEGE:

INGREDIENTS FOR ANGER

throbbing
 pulse, twitching hands
hasty
 steps, flushing face,
stir
 once counter-clockwise.

speeding thoughts, crowded mouth
tapping
 foot, parched tongue--
don't forget the frog's eyes.

Erika Buiter
Ireton, IA
Dordt College, Sioux City

HOT COCOA

Sweet-popped, serene,
Fresh as quail feet.
Splendid as pie,
Long locks of tossed dream.
Heavy steam, comfy seat,
Warm blanket and socks.
Now curl up and sip,
Glean riddles long dropped.

Kendra Nydam
Mitchell, SD
Dordt College, Sioux City

CALIFORNIA WILDFIRE

Even the summer sky
In the middle of nowhere
Had a hue
Of red sun-fire purples
And the smoke of
California weeds
Remained embedded
In our lungs

Anna Keil
West Linn, OR
University of Iowa, Iowa City

FIRST PLACE, HIGH SCHOOL:

DISSECTED EARS

Four years old, "accommodate", discriminate
Classroom horror, teachers hide—don't cooperate
Friends whisper, left out again
Telephone game, not my best friend

Words mix together, they blend and get chopped
They are dissected in my ears

I ask you to repeat, over, and over, and over again
Until your lips grow weary and your patience turns on you
But you have to understand: you need to try too

I try and grasp the other side, where voices are clear
"never mind"—not a common phrase

Thousands of lips jumping around, airplane noises, random sounds

Ask me a question, unheard of, unknown
No answer from me, why? I should have known—no

I read that wrong, your lips aren't like a book
Words aren't written upon a page

They are in the air, on the face, inside my hands-which you can't comprehend
Hands like birds; flying, jumping, painting pictures from thin air, I understand

Breathe in, breathe out

Finally, I know who I am

Katelyn Donnelly, Grade 12
Shenandoah High School, Shenandoah
Kathryn Freed, Teacher

GONE

Hugging you was like hugging smoke.
I could see you and I could feel you,
but you were never really there.

Clarissa Huisman, Grade 10
Osage High School, Osage
Melanie Gast, Teacher

SECOND PLACE, HIGH SCHOOL:

HIDDEN IN THE ORCHARD

There was a sweet smell of citrus
Accompanied by a slight hum of birds
And a soft, colorful beauty
To distract me.

He brought me so that our worries
Would be hidden by the trees
And the leaves would droop over my eyes,
Covering the cries.

He took my hand and I went stiff
Because his body was not mine.
It now belonged to the other woman
With whom he slept.

But I was forever his,
As my ring had always known,
So I hid the truth inside
To be a good wife.

Kaua'i Cua, Grade 9
Valley Southwoods, West Des Moines
Christie Wicks, Teacher

THIRD PLACE, HIGH SCHOOL:

FEAR

What is fear?
Fear is red and blue lights,
An officer with an angry face.
Fear is the click of cuffs on your wrist.
It's being thrown into the back of the car.
Fear is looking at the fence separating you from the front.
It's not being able to tell your dad what's happening,
The tears running down my face.
Fear is watching your brother and sister fight for you.
It's breaking your wrist trying to call your dad,
watching your mom smile as it's happening.
Fear is finally realizing your mom doesn't care.
Fear is how you feel without your dad.

Skyler Freeman, Grade 11
Boyer Valley High School, Dunlap
Mrs. K. Johnson, Teacher

FIRST HONORABLE MENTION, HIGH SCHOOL:

COMMON THINGS

People's heads are low and calm
The traffic in the street was flying.
A predictable change in traffic lights.
It's the exact same day again.

A tall building stands in one building.
The computer screen is flashing.
Countless fingers typed quickly on the keyboard.
Do what all of us are doing.

The same thing, a different day.
Different people, the same thing.

The expression was overflowing in their faces.
Tired, numb, confused
The heart is lonely and helpless, but it is impossible to confide
Had to be forced to surrender to reality.

Richard Hu, Grade 11
Saint Albert Schools, Council Bluffs
Ann Coombs, Teacher

SECOND HONORABLE MENTION, HIGH SCHOOL:

A SON AND HIS FATHER

A son and his father
Bathed in the golden glow of the setting sun
Throw a baseball back and forth
On the freshly cut grass
Of the baseball diamond
Kicking up dust
In early May
I can't help but feel
That this is what Heaven
Must be like

Tabetha DeGroot, Grade12
Faith Christian Home School, Sioux Center
Twila DeGroot, Teacher

THIRD HONORABLE MENTION, HIGH SCHOOL:

VIRTUAL REALITY

How has it come to be
We've lost our sense of creativity
For the time spent in reality
Is less than it looks to be
Staring down at a phone
To pick it up as we're more prone
Watching all day TV
How has it come to be
We live in a virtual reality
Obsessed with liking and following
Video games take up all your time, shopping at home Amazon Prime
Dating behind a screen, ignoring the fact that you need to clean
Multi-task quick and fast, staying up all night you never rest
Cyberbullies drive kids to death, online you can sell anonymous meth
Live cams of murder and nudity, the web teaches young kids crudity
Turning kids to apathetic tykes
Why are we discouraged by dislikes
Desensitized by violence on TV
We live in a virtual reality

Ashleigh Manders, Grade 9
Prairie Point Middle School, Cedar Rapids
Denise Roth, Teacher

I AM A CRAZY/DANGEROUS GUY

I am a crazy/dangerous guy that loves cars
I wonder what death is like
I hear the roar of an engine
I see the sadness in my family's eyes
I am a crazy/dangerous guy that loves cars

I pretend that I will make a difference
I feel the pain of a boy without his father
I touch the cool water on a hot summer's day
I worry I will be alone
I cry for those who are lost
I am a crazy/dangerous guy who loves cars

I understand the world isn't fair
I say the lord is our solution
I dream of a world with my father
I try to do my best
I am a crazy/dangerous guy who loves cars

Quinten Julian, Grade 9
Saint Albert Schools, Council Bluffs
Ann Coombs, Teacher

THE TRUTH YOU'RE AFRAID TO ASK FOR

At the front of the room, my English teacher holds her roll sheet.
Smith. Easy. *Jones.* Simple. *Schneider.* Not even a pause.

What stops her steady procession is three little syllables. *Ri-ve-ra.*

She is not a mean woman, my English teacher,
but those sounds just don't seem to meld with her tongue.

She tries once. *Revira*? My name has become a question.
Were it not for it, there would be little proof of my muddied heritage.

Her mouth screws up. She doubts herself. Another attempt. *Riviera?*
I'm pale enough to pass, and I have no culture that comes up in conversation.

Certainty has yet to make itself known.
The tell tale uptick betraying her cluelessness holds firm.

Then—*Riveria.*
Where these extra vowels come from is beyond me.
Six letters escape the grasp of a college-educated woman.

I love the name she struggles over, the name people blink twice
before fitting with my appearance.

Rivera.

My correction is swift, ending the butchering of a single word, and she's quick
to move on down the list to my less confusing classmates.

She will be happy to find that none of their names need answers.

Bella Rivera, Grade 10
Ankeny Centennial High School, Ankeny
Teresa Lawler, Teacher

HANDS

Your wrinkled hands
And ring-stacked fingers
Wrote in smooth cursive handwriting
Nimble hands calculated all the bills
Adding and subtracting to the very penny
With fingernails polished bright coral between your teeth
Biting nervously but unknowingly, making all of us smile
Your hand patted my cheek on our last Thanksgiving together
And I'm thankful for these memories, because I see them every day
So I always feel your hands are
Guiding the way

Molly Wright, Grade 11
Valley High School, West Des Moines
Blythe Stanfel, Teacher

I AM FROM

I am from Palo Beach
From The Grizzlies and The Tigers.
I am from the raisin bread my granny makes,
each bite sweeter than the last.
I am from the flowers that only bloomed in spring.
I am from the flowers that only bloomed in spring.

I'm from birthdays and silliness.
From Jasmine and Israel and laughing till my tummy hurts.
From no's and yes's.
I'm from the bible and church.
I'm from Granny Josie and apple pie,
from the greenhouse with the red Lincoln.

I am from long drives with the breeze on my face.

Ja'Lyrial Briggs, Grade 11
Prairie Point Middle School, Cedar Rapids
Denise Roth, Teacher

QUIET WINTER

Once Fall has faded
Winter will come
Bringing cold and snow
But also a quiet no other season can bring

It's nighttime
And everything is blanketed in white
So quiet, so still
It's so peaceful

There is no snap of twigs being broken
No animals move
The cold is like a preservative
Everything in suspended animation

I stand out here, waiting for everything to awake
While no wind howls through the cold night air
And silent snow falling with the lightest of a touch

Soon the spring will come, breaking the quiet
Everything will be bustling
There will be no more snow to hold everything together

This awed silence is everything in one word
This cold is nothing to the quiet of winter

Autumn Schlichtmann, Grade 10
Gladbrook-Reinbeck High School, Reinbeck
Angie Miller, Teacher

RAIN

The rain,
oh, the sweet rain
kiss the rooftops
a small patter
a drummer playing an original
wake me up in the morning
to find a day that is dim
where the leaves sigh under the droplets
where the world is quiet and at ease
wake me up to a stream
that cascades down my window
wake me up to a morning
where the minds are at rest
where the people are quiet and thoughtful
let me wake up to
rain
when the heavens open up
and nature pours out

                            Emily Irmen, Grade 9
               Prairie Point Middle School, Cedar Rapids
                              Denise Roth, Teacher

SNAPSHOT

In a snapshot
a mountainous terrain
blanketed with towering forest of pines
which from afar
resembles toothpicks sprouting from the ground
the opening reveals a lake
motionless
with a muddy reflection of the trees
smudges of white paint the blue sky
frozen in time.
If you step into the picture
mountains appear steep
taller than any skyscraper
coated with lanky firs
in the window of trees
the water ripples from the cool summer breeze
and shimmers from the rays of sun
wispy white clouds and tall looming pines
reflect a blurred image like a mirror.

                        Hailey Butterwegge, Grade 11
               Valley High School, West Des Moines
                            Blythe Stanfel, Teacher

AT WHAT COST?

At what cost will it take you to realize that once all the trees are gone your finest pieces of literature cannot be written on money
At what cost will it take you to realize that once the ocean has vanished behind plastic you cannot bathe yourself in money
At what cost will it take to realize that once you devour every last drop of palm oil you can not devour money
At what cost will it take you to realize that once your water sources are filled with oil you can not quench your thirst with money
At what cost will it take you to realize that once the water spills over you cannot build a life raft with money
At what cost will it take you to realize that once a captive animal takes their last breath you cannot be entertained with money
At what will it take you to realize that once everything is gone all you have is money

Reagan Wilson, Grade 9
Prairie Point Middle School, Cedar Rapids
Denise Roth, Teacher

WHAT HAPPENS WHEN WE DIE?

What happens when we die I don't know but what I do know it's not just us closing our eyes seeing Nothing but black maybe We go back doing a restart Or having another start With a different ship Going through the same Old little crazy trip With a different back story Going through different categories But who knows life after death Not all these fable religions But that's your decision To hear the preacher and listen All I need is to do is to learn Through my mistake all through my days the good I give That's how my god forgives The sins I make So all the bad and evil in my Life he always takes away Even though I know my body decays I never forget my soul always flies away

DeShawn Stepter, Grade 11
Oskaloosa High School, Oskaloosa
Lauren Ernst, Teacher

THE RUNWAY

Down this runway

The sun has never been louder

My walk was never so focused

Designer has never been prouder

Handcrafted down to each seam

So much time within these sleeves

Sliding in love when I slipped on these pants

She unstitched all these feelings with her hands.

Joel Garcia, Grade 12
Valley High School, West Des Moines
Blythe Stanfel, Teacher

SCHOOL SYSTEM

Taking away creativity and identity.
Turning kids into robots.
Making kids believe they are not smart!
For seven hours a day, we are told what to think.
And grades are just a competition.
Look at us, being taught about rocks, and 1+1=2.
Do you not realize the world is changing.
We need people who think creatively, and innovatively.
We have new jobs, new technology.
We don't have to learn the same way as we used to.
But wait it gets worse!
Teachers stand before 25 kids when each kid
has different strengths and different needs
And they teach us all the same way.
It doesn't make sense!
But at the same time, teachers do so much for us yet they are underpaid.
They spend hours a day dealing with troublesome students,
Staying up far too late at night grading papers.
Not only that but sometimes
Teachers are able to reach into the heart of that student
and allow the student to find themselves.
It's time for a change.

Aiden Roemig, Grade 9
Prairie Point Middle School, Cedar Rapids
Denise Roth, Teacher

WHY I FEAR NOTHING

Night
is not a thing
but an absence of.
The Darkness
that hides in most people,
that overwhelms some,
does not leak in;
The Light drains out,
Shadows
are not a being;
they are lonely places
lacking Love,
because something bigger than them
stole their Light.
I
do not fear a thing.
I fear
the lacking of.

Megan Kaufmann, Grade 12
Hempstead High School, Dubuque
Michelle Hunt, Teacher

THE SERENITY OF THE SNOW

The serenity of the sow
makes it unbearable
to disturb
the sincere silence
that carries in the wind.

The sheet of snow
undisturbed is enough
to make one cry for every
sinister step they take ruins
the sublime sea of snow.

The subtle stillness
in the air makes
it appear as though
seconds stutter and turn
into hours.

Allison Narmi, Grade 9
Saint Albert Schools, Council Bluffs
Ann Coombs, Teacher

FIRST PLACE, UPPER GRADES:

THE OIL PAINTING OF HER LIFE

It starts with a blue sky,
Frogs croaking and birds a-fly.

Fields full of lavender,
The scent in the air,
But a breeze just strong enough to blow
The wind through your hair.

A distant hum of a clarinet near,
But so soft, you must hush in order to hear.

The land so bright,
All day and all night,
The air with no hue,
Just color, and white.

No engine when you listen quietly,
But a bit of conflict just mere.

Her life like a painting,
With details you can only see from near.

Kira Taylor, Grade 7
South Middle School, Waukee
Mrs. Patterson, Teacher

WATER

You're crystal clear, like a diamond ring.
I bathe in you to
Keep myself clean.
I drink you to
Stay alive.
Thank you, water, for helping me survive.

Talyn Strovers, Grade 7
North Polk Middle School, Alleman
Steve Leach, Teacher

DOG WALK

Taking my dog for a walk
Can be very stressful
She'll go to strangers and talk
About how she is so wonderful.

Rianne Van Meeteren, Grade 6
Sanborn Christian School, Sanborn
Sam De Groot, Teacher

SECOND PLACE, UPPER GRADES:

MAKING $20 OFF A SIMPLE CHORE

When I was just six,
Just a young child,
My dad and I knew there was a furnace to fix.
My Job was quite mild.
Then there was a part my dad could not do.
A spot too tight for a grown man like he.
He said to me, "Hunter, can you fit through?"
"But it is dirty, and moldy! Why on earth me?"
"I will give you five dollars, if you give it a try."
"But I am scared there are monsters, with very sharp teeth."
"How about ten dollars, so you do not cry?"
"What about twenty? I'll go underneath for sure!"
"I suppose, as long as it's done."
So underneath I went in the long, dark pit.
I untangled wires one by one.
My dad was very happy, I didn't throw a fit.
I made twenty dollars on a five dollar deal.
I would be happy, and Dad would be elated.
I was happy because I made one heck of a steal.
And my dad was most proud for the time he had waited!

Hunter Shipley, Grade 8
Burlington Notre Dame, Burlington
Esther Waterman, Teacher

THIRD PLACE, UPPER GRADES:

WHAT A PANE

English is such a pane

Eye get a F on every assignment

Why do the rules have to be sew confusing

I dont know what wood be worse,

Swallowing glass or setting in class.

Lily Hofman, Grade 8
Sanborn Christian School, Sanborn
Sam De Groot, Teacher

FIRST HONORABLE MENTION, UPPER GRADES:

INSPIRATION

Under a gray sky

A pail carries me away

I can see the stars

Miya Krueger, Grade 5
Sawyer Elementary, Ames
Mark Royer, Teacher

SECOND HONORABLE MENTION, UPPER GRADES:

UNFAIR

Life is unfair now

This existence is pointless

My computer died

Ian WIlliamson, Grade 5
Sawyer Elementary, Ames
Mark Royer, Teacher

THIRD HONORABLE MENTION, UPPER GRADES:

ART

It slashes, it splats, and goes this way and that

It creates an image that looks cool or wack

But it doesn't matter if it's good or bad

You're an artist now, appreciate that

Sam Hostetter, Grade 5
Edwards Elementary, Ames
Mark Royer, Teacher

HUNTING OWLS

Swooping over snow
In the quietest of flight
Hunting owls fly

Kelsey Robinson, Grade 5
Sawyer Elementary, Ames
Mark Royer, Teacher

THE RIVER

The river flowing by
A fish jumping makes a splash
Silence once again

Sarah Higgins, Grade 5
Edwards Elementary, Ames
Mark Royer, Teacher

WINTER

Snow falls in blankets
The trees sparkle with beauty
Everything is white

Adeline Mund, Grade 5
Sawyer Elementary, Ames
Mark Royer, Teacher

BABY SISTER

To the hospital
waiting, waiting, waiting, then
I hear her first cry

Lola Austin, Grade 7
North Polk Middle School, Alleman
Steve Leach, Teacher

WITH BOTH HEADPHONES IN

Nothing else matters.
Every stress is gone.
Every worry is absent.
All I think about are the poetic lyrics,
The somber piano notes or the ecstatic drum beats.
With both headphones in,
I'm far in my own world.
Far from my stress,
Far from my anxiety,
Music lets me escape.
With both headphones in,
Nothing else matters.

Abby French, Grade 8
Saint Albert Schools, Council Bluffs
Ann Coombs, Teacher

ANGER

anger is
consuming
like a fire

anger is
destroying
like a flood

anger is
contagious
like the plague

Adelle Wolfswinkel, Grade 8
Sanborn Christian School, Sanborn
Sam DeGroot, Teacher

COLORS

They can be so bright and vivid
With no texture and no ridges
They can tell a story with no mouth
They can be everywhere both North and South
Colors can make your eyes pop
Or let you take a break and stop
Sometimes they can even make you feel loved
And many other things we're unaware of

William Bielefeld, Grade 6
Osage Middle School, Osage
Meaghan Johnson, Teacher

THE TOWERS

The terror and the sadness,
The joy for those who escaped the madness.
The day that made America cry,
But our spirit will never die.
We sat inside our homes disbelieving,
While our hope began leaving.
The survivors we were rejoicing,
But that loss of hope from our minds we are forcing.
The planes' impact shook like an earthquake,
But we had no idea how many lives that it would take.
Our spirit of joy leaving us behind,
The sadness we felt for every body that we would find.
The activity made a sound like a buzz,
It was undeniable the disaster it was.
Today we remember those lost lives, beautiful like flowers,
Remembering those lost inside the towers.

Nathan Edwards, Grade 8
Burlington Notre Dame, Burlington
Esther Waterman, Teacher

HOW COULD THEY EVER SEE IT COMING

They were worried
They were scared
They were hung up by despair

They were burning
They were falling
How could they ever see it coming?

Dust was everywhere
Lives were taken
They are missed
They will always be remembered
In our hearts and prayers
How could they ever see it coming?
How could they ever have known?
Where are their sons and daughters now?
Living life alone.

Tianna Lovell, Grade 8
Burlington Notre Dame, Burlington
Esther Waterman, Teacher

GROWING UP

I remember when you'd read to me.
You'd smile as you read.
I'd soak up all the information.
Why do we have to grow up?

I remember when you would play games with me.
You'd sit and laugh at me,
while I made up a new game.
But, Mom, why did those times have to leave?

I remember when we'd put on music
and dance together. Afterward, you'd
hug me and tell me not to grow up.
Mom, why did I have to anyway?

Alex Clover, Grade 7
East Marshall Middle School, Gilman
Mrs. Heishman, Teacher

PETRIFIED

I am petrified
By permineralization
Wood or stone
Or something else entirely
A fossil
The effects of
Mother Nature's magic spell
Cast upon me
Forcing me to stand there
Petrified
Staring, spellbound
At a rainbow of elements
Iron oxides and manganese
Cobalt and carbon
Mixed together in a single enchanting concept
That could only exist by magic
By a spell
By nature.

Kate Carlson, Grade 6
Saint Francis of Assisi School, West Des Moines
Jenny Umstead, Teacher

PRODIGY

A term that had been tagged on them years ago
No longer seemed a shiny badge of pride
Instead it was a cardboard sign
Now labeled "nerd"

Athena XiMeng Wu, Grade 7
Northwest Junior High, Coralville
Brooke Freund, Teacher

FIRST PLACE, LOWER GRADES:

DIARY

Diamond in my house but worthless to robbers
Images of daily life
A safe for my memory
Reading to replay
Yesterday once more

Kryos Yuefam Wu, Grade 3
Van Allen Elementary, North Liberty
Tammy Bell, Teacher

SECOND PLACE, LOWER GRADES:

PUMPKINS ARE REALLY NICE

Pumpkin pie, pumpkin spice
Making pumpkin bread with Mom is really nice

Trip to the patch, pick off the vine
Don't carve your jack-o-lantern until it is time!

Conor McMahon, Grade 4
Jordan Creek Elementary, West Des Moines
Mrs. Flagg, Teacher

THIRD PLACE, LOWER GRADES:

ROSES

Roses are red
Red is said
Said is sad
Sad is mad
Mad is plaid
Plaid is bad

Zaylin Harden-Barrow, Grade 3
Edwards Elementary, Ames
Mark Royer, Teacher

FIRST HONORABLE MENTION, LOWER GRADES:

OUCH

I ran into it
It was your glass whiteboard
Was it expensive?

Brendan Stanley, Grade 3
Edwards Elementary, Ames
Mark Royer, Teacher

SECOND HONORABLE MENTION, LOWER GRADES:

LISTEN

Do you need glasses?
Do you need health care?
Do you even listen to me?

Corwyn Evans, Grade 3
Edwards Elementary, Ames
Mark Royer, Teacher

THIRD HONORABLE MENTION, LOWER GRADES:

BIRDS IN THE SKY

Fly high in the sky
over houses and buildings
landing on a roof

Allison Roman Resendiz, Grade 2
Rolling Green Elementary, Urbandale
Ms. J Bowie, Teacher

FALL

Down the leaves   go ... crunch!
Many colors beautiful
WInter's coming soon!

Parker Dewey, Grade 2
Rolling Green Elementary, Urbandale
Julie Bowie, Teacher

STAY UP ALL NIGHT

When the stars come out, some are planets
I like to see their shapes and colors
I lie in the grass and I pet my dogs
We look up and we dream
About what it would be like
To ride a rocket to the sky

Logan McMahon, Kindergarten
Jordan Creek Elementary, West Des Moines
Mrs. Farrell, Teacher

KITTY CAT KATE

Kitty Cat Kate is always late
She works at the store in the fashion shop galore
Her greatest fear is ... DEER!

CeCe Appleton, Grade 3
Sawyer Elementary, Ames
Mark Royer, Teacher

CROCODILES

Snapping jaws ... scary!
Living in a river ... wet!
Insanely big ... EEK!

Paxton Chancellor, Grade2
Rolling Green Elementary, Urbandale
Julie Bowie, Teacher

MY SHELL

Shells can be curvy
or bumpy,
with little holes like a
dotted blanket
on the bed
waiting for a snuggle
It looks like
a circle rolling
around for playing.

Cora Laird, Grade 2
Rolling Green Elementary, Urbandale
Julie Bowie, Teacher

ANIMALS

Animals beautiful some have dots
Like a color on
A quilt orange like
A tiger yellow like
A lion some animals

Jump out of the ocean
Like humpback whale splashing
everywhere

Live everywhere are different kinds
Some live in
Land and water
Some live in swamps like alligators

Jin Schroeder, Grade 2
Rolling Green Elementary, Urbandale
Miss K Berg, Teacher

THE ROOM

In the dark room
A large boom occurs
As the fire goes fwoom
Sometimes you wonder
Why you went into this room

Alex Mudryk, Grade 3
Edwards Elementary, Ames
Mark Royer, Teacher

FLOWER FEELINGS

Rose, loved
Sunflower, different
Almond, rare
Blossom, beautiful
Poppy, neon
Bell Flower, dazzling
Passion Dahlia, sweet, light
Lily, awesome
Tulip, grateful
Orchid, sweet
Lotus, special
Petunia, silly
Peony, smell good, cool
Daffodil, bright
Daisy, happy

Gracelyn Cottingham, Grade 3
Marcus-Meriden-Cleghorn School, Marcus
Jodi Feser, Teacher

HAIKU

Winter is happy.

Sugar cookies baking time

Snow on top of rug

Renee Cook, Grade 4
Briggs Elementary, Maquoketa
Rebecca Benedix, Teacher

ELEPHANT

My elephant
ate a peanut
last night
in my bright pink bed.
He was hungry
because he was working out.

Lauren Feldmann, Grade 4
North Polk Central Elementary, Alleman
Marcy Donelson, Teacher

SCHOOL

School is like
A kids's
Lounge
With

Teachers
And
Guidance
Counselors

With
Art teachers

Colton Mears, Grade 2
Rolling Green Elementary, Urbandale
Miss K Berg, Teacher

SOCCER

It is black and white
You can always kick the ball
It is the best sport

Brian Rivera-Perez, Grade 2
Rolling Green Elementary, Urbandale
Miss K Berg, Teacher

INDEX

ADULTS:

A
Abramowitz, Janvier...45
Allen, Joyce..............138
Ambrose, Janine........98
Andersen, Lila L.........52
Anderson, Tami..........16
Andorf, Michael..........69
Armstrong, Mark.......114
Arsanjani, Ali..............88
Ashmore, Alyssa........74
Augustson, LaVonne..60

B
Baker, Sheila..............37
Bannister, Margot.......36
Barker, Ethel..............65
Anna Barnes............144
Baszczynski, Marilyn..26
Bayles, Mike..............51
Behlke, Donna.........126
Benda, Jo Ann.........116
Bengston, Anthony A 100
Benzing, Diane.........123
Berhow, Mary L..........85
Berryhill, Allison........120
Bieber, Pat...............132
Blankenburg, Jan.....135
Blomgren, Pamela J...36
Bloom, Barbara..........31
Boal, Beverly..............62
Boettcher, Norbe B.....66
Bolin, Mary...............117
Bonham, Catherine....54
Borton, Pauline........132
Bowman, John...........54
Braddy, Glen..............95
Bradway, PJ.............109
Branson, Janet........104
Brant, Betsy.............103
Brayton, Stephen.......98
Brink, Christine........122
Brockmeyer, Lloyd.....44
Brockshus, Roger......60
Bubendorfer, Phoebe.30
Buck, Patricia............92
Butz, Sarah A.............43

C
Cabada, Caroliena.....27
Cadwallader, Iola P....47
Cardamon, Barbara...34
Carlson, Maxine.........78
Carr, Karen................82
Carter, Brianna..........63
Case, Thomas...........44
Cavanagh, Lynn.........57
Cavanagh, Erin..........89
Chambers, Joe..........66
Christy, Kathy Geren..73
Clark, Heather A........46
Clark, Shelly J............55
Clover, Mary..............61
Clute, Kelly R.............17
Clutter, Alanna.........138
Cochran, Angie..........73
Coffeen, Adrienne......76
Collins, Patti.............114
Collinson, John W......26
Conard, Margot..........87
Conover, Jean C.......21
Crouse, Emily..........107
Curran, Justin............32

D
Daftari, Maryam.........95
Dall, William...............56
Danner, Ellen G.......118
DeFrance Duffy.........45
De Jong, Fred W.....101
Derr-Smith, Heather...25
Deyoe, Sandy............23
DeYoung, Emily.......123
Dohlman, Marjorie.....59
Dolphin, Linda..........106
Dorn, Andrea.............89
Dovel, Kim...............146
Dovenspike, Vicky...139
Doyle, Shea...............18
Drake, Sue.................40
Durdan, Paul..............77
Durkin, Theresa.........53

E
Edens, Tracy............128
Elsbecker, Rose.......113
Emmons, Julie Sharp.39
Erickson, Elaine.........33
Evans, Angela............34
Evans, Jean M.........130

F
Faulkner, Matthew.....68
Felleman, Laura.........61
Fischels, Michael.......35
Fladlien, Mike............58
Friestad-Tate, Jill.....102
Fudge, Edy..............119

G
Gardner, Esther M.....79
Georgou, Thomas......72
Gilbaugh, Milli..........131
Gilchrist, Janet E......145
Gillespie, Marylyn L..117
Gingerich, Tom..........31
Glad, Dorothy E.......112
Gordon, Lee L..........124
Gradwohl, David M....77
Graeser, Bill...............20
Green, Beverly Mattix.51
Green, Sandra L......109
Grover, Tim...............71
Gustafson, Judy A.....90

H
Haakenson, Marcia....33
Hahn, Tyler..............132
Hanaman, Nancy.....143
Hanson, Patrick.........67
Harper, Kass..............76
Harris, Lori C.............34
Harris, Phyllis IT......135
Hart, Kathleen U......140
Hasenmiller, David.....49
Haywood, Bill............83
Hengst, II, H Randall.143
Hesford, Brad............79
Hibbing, Josie..........130
Hibma, Rachel K........28
Hill, Viola...................99
Hilton, Shirley...........128
Hinnen, Robert M......48
Hoeg, LeAnn.............97
Hoover, Lorene..........28
Hoskinson, Rob.........84
Hovland, Annette M..144
Hudson, William E...113
Humston, Mary J.....116
Huxsol, Patricia.........37

I
Irwin, Ranelle.............45

J
Jacobson, Roberta...133
Jass, Kerrin R..........133

Johnson, Julie Allyn 130
Johnston, Carole 105
Joyce, Daniel F 35
Justus, Allison Boyd.......14

K
Kahl, Ronald 96
Kanago, Dixie 70
Kitzmiller, Jean 58
Kladivo, Karen 22
Klein, Susan 14
Knox, Zachary 58
Kolacia, Nathan 80
Kramer, Lynn 80
Kutchen, Frank.............119

L
LaBella, Teresa 83
Ladegaard, Sandra 116
Lamphier, MaryJane 91
Larson, Rustin 23
Lawler, Teresa 56
Leach, Stephen E 64
Lewin, Rita...................133
Lewis, Deborah............129
Lockey, Jill 66
Lofgren, Kelcy................71
Logan, Jan.....................51
Lucas, Mark S..............108
Lyle, Joy.........................86
Lyle, Levi........................30

M
Mackey, Matilda SC........19
Magee, Jed 131
Mann, Reagan 59
Mathis, Dorothy 32
Maulsby, Dennis 127
McCargar, Les 54
McKim, Cleo 142
McMahon, Sean 88
McManus, Mary E........103
McMullen, Carol B 39
Medema, Betty............110
Meyer, Jeffrey 134
Meyer, JoAnn 111
Meyer, Kathy................106
Millard, Joe 134
Miller, Douglas L 46
Miller, Marty 27
Mitchell, John.................63
Moe, Patricia K 103
Moore, Dan 13
Moore, Marjorie W 65

Morse, Ramona 136
Mortenson, Virginia......130
Moss, Donnella 29
Moss. Mary Sue.............67
Mueller, Audrey 70
Muhlenbruch, Melba 118
Muller, Linda MJ 38
Myers, Jan 37

N
Narland, Jerrold 42
Nash, Linda M 68
Netherton, Dale 139
Newman, Merle E 100
Nicholas, Anna...............48
Nickerson, Nolan D........38
Noeth, Patricia E..........129
Nolan, Judy....................50

O
Obermueller, Nancy 112
Olney, Angela.................94
Osland, Susan F 84
Ostedgaard, Robin 137
Ostroff, Frann...............101
Overocker, Terry 78

P
Padden, Ginnie 60
Pannhoff, Carole............53
Paul, Linda E 62
Pearce, Floyd 42
Permann, Mary L...........50
Perry, Bill........................75
Peters, Nancy J 74
Peterson, Mary 82
Petri, Lauren 20
Phillips, Jeremiah 35
Piconi, Gabriella 131
Primus, Bailey................93

R
Ralston, Delia 13
Rammelsberg, Joan.....118
Ramsey, Richard R......127
Reed, Rita F 81
Reeves, Rodney 104
Reid, Carolyn Yates......111
Reinecke, Warren R 125
Riddle, William P..........109
Riggan, Nancy 115
Ringold, Lucy.................82
Robbins, Lynn..............144
Roberts, Hollie 97
Roberts, Jerry 88

Roelfsema, Kathryn ...64
Rohr, Gene R 136
Rohrbaugh, Carolyn.140
Rosazza, Trudi...........49
Rose, Steve 25
Roth, Denise 108
Roth, James.............102
Russell, Kathleen........99

S
Sabelka, Paul C 72
Sandvik, Myrna 77
Schar, Joanne D 127
Schiotis, Mary 93
Schmitt, Karen 142
Schoenewe, Nancy 92
Schroeder, Larry 55
Schuster, Valrie 147
Sears, Rick.................80
Shannon, Lori...........122
Shaw, Robert 21
Shivvers, Linda 145
Signori, Jacqueline...110
Simmons, Bill 131
Sisterman, Carol 75
Sly-Terpstra, Dawn.....24
Smith, Angela.............69
Smith, Brianna 137
Smith, Lindsey 141
Smolik, Margaret........86
Snethen, John 147
Sohl-Cryer, Laura.....121
Sprafka, Robin 15
Spratt, Elizabeth.......128
Squires, Ron E...........85
Stahl, DIck..................16
Stauffer, Kathleen.......15
Steinbach, Robert 29
Stenzel, Eleanor.......124
Stevenson, JoAn 47
Stone, Crystal 18
Stone, Janis K..........146
Stromberg, Audrey.....22
Sullivan, Marie 105
Suter, Margaret Flint ..17

T
Tabbert, Bryan..........133
Tallman, Alma...........107
Taylor, Betty 120
Taylor, Cory B............41
Thedens, Lisa Ross ...41
Thieman, Shelly R....129
Thoen, Helen J.........117
Thomann, Kay..........143

Thompson, Laura.....141
Thomson, Jean..........113
Turner, Del Todey.....131
Turner, Michelle..........83

U
Underwood, Pat.........24

V
Vallier, Marvin D..........96
Vesely, Suzanne A......81
Vondrak, Jayne R.......19
Vos, Madison..............87

W
Wallarab, Richard K...61
Wambold, Robert D....40
Wambold, Robert D....43
Waske, Joan Jessen..90
Watts, Margery L........91
Weaver, Val.................94
Westbrook, Virginia..132
Westvold, Margaret....57
Wheeler, Barbara B....71
Whitmore, Rebecca...73
Wiener, Janet............129
Willging, Laura..........132
Wilson, Lucille M.......125
Wilson, Mike...............63
Wolfe, Linda.............121
Wolfe, Norman..........118
Wyrick, Shirley...........52

Y
Yoak, Martha..............49
Young, Sally J...........115

Z
Zimmerman, Jill..........56
Zotalis, Lynne.............30

STUDENTS:

A
Adams, Hannah.......150
Appleton, CeCe........171
Austin, Lola..............165

B
Bielefeld, William......166
Bousema, Katie........150
Briggs, Ja'Lyrial........157
Buiter, Erika..............151
Butterwegge, Hailey.158

C
Carlson, Kate...............168
Chancellor, Paxton......171
Clover, Alex..................168
Cook, Renee................173
Cottingham, Gracelyn..173
Cua, Kaua'i..................153

D
DeGroot, Tabetha........154
Dewey, Parker.............171
Donnelly, Katelyn.........152
Donstad, Anneliese......149

E
Edwards, Nathan..........167
Evans, Corwyn.............170

F
Feldmann, Lauren.......173
Freeman, Skyler..........153
French, Abby...............166

G
Garcia, Joel.................160

H
Harden-Barrow, Zaylin.169
Higgins, Sarah.............165
Hofman, Lily.................163
Hostetter, Sam.............164
Hu, Richard..................154
Huisman, Clarissa.......152

I
Irmen, Emily.................158

J
Julian, Quinten.............155

K
Kaufmann, Megan.......161
Keil, Anna....................151
Kochuyt, Ashley...........150
Krueger, Miya..............164

L
Laird, Cora...................172
Lovell, Tianna..............167

M
Manders, Ashleigh.......155
McMahon, Conor.........169
McMahon, Logan.........171
Mears, Colton..............174

Mudryk, Alex.................172
Mund, Adeline..............165

N
Narmi, Allison...............161
Nicol, Albie...................148
Nydam, Kendra............151

R
Resendiz, Allison R......170
Rivera, Bella.................156
Rivera-Perez, Brian.....174
Robinson, Kelsey.........165
Roemig, Aiden.............160

S
Schlichtmann, Autumn.157
Schroeder, Jin..............172
Schultz, Danielle..........149
Shipley, Hunter.............163
Stanley, Brendan.........170
Stepter, DeShawn........159
Strovers, Talyn.............162

T
Taylor, Kira...................162

V
Van Meeteren, Rianne.162

W
Williamson, Ian............164
Wilson, Reagan...........159
Wind, Anneke..............148
Wolfswinkel, Adelle......166
Wright, Molly................156
Wu, Athena XiMeng.....168
Wu, Kyros Yuefan........169